The Trauma Effect

The Trauma Effect

Published by The Conrad Press Ltd. in the United
Kingdom 2023

Tel: +44(0)1227 472 874

www.theconradpress.com
info@theconradpress.com

ISBN 978-1-915494-84-9

Typesetting and cover design by Michelle Emerson
michelleemerson.co.uk

The Conrad Press logo was designed by Maria Priestley.

Printed and bound in Great Britain by Clays Ltd,
Elcograf S.p.A

The Trauma Effect

Exploring and resolving
inherited trauma

Zetta Thomelin

I dedicate this book to the memory of Keith, Graham and Carol who once lived, but who died much too young and who have been hidden in the dark for far too long.

Also by Zetta Thomelin

Books

The Healing Metaphor – Hypnotherapy Scripts
Self-Help? Self-Hypnosis!

Audio

Journeys into Nature
Avebury and Silbury Hill
Sleep
Journey into Sleep
Relieve Stress

Contents

Introduction

I wonder if there is a trauma tucked away in *your* family?

It could be your own experience, or something that has affected someone else, even from long ago.

Trauma will often ripple out into a family and affect far more than those directly involved, creating a problem that can last generations.

There is a trauma in my family, a hidden trauma.

I wanted to know more about it. I wanted to shine a light on what had remained concealed beneath a shroud of shame and consider the ways it may have affected me. This book reflects that journey from its first tentative steps to ultimately, a deep sense of resolution and understanding.

I am telling you my story both to understand it better and to help you to understand yours.

Much has been written about the impact of trauma, but when I began to investigate the idea of generational trauma - the trauma within families that, in effect, gets handed down from one generation to another, and so on - I realised at once that there was much less written about that. The old skeleton in the family cupboard which nobody can talk about can have a huge impact on the health of a family both physical and psychological. This is trauma that is subconsciously gifted to you, so you are not necessarily aware that it is impacting on you, especially if the trauma happened before you were born.

At first, I began writing about generational trauma so I could understand it better for myself. But I soon realised that I wanted to create something readable and relatable to help other people, too, understand this concept of trauma passing down through generations, to help them to halt it and encourage them to address their family issues. I felt well placed to turn my work into something to help others.

As a therapist, having worked with trauma across a range of areas with my clients, telling my own story is somewhat exposing, and many therapists would shy away from such public scrutiny. But if this book helps someone else out there, even if it is just one person, then it has all been worthwhile.

Storytelling is a highly effective way to communicate ideas and to affect healing. I wanted to integrate this within a therapeutic journey. It is like one giant case study which can provide insight upon the subject for anyone who has experienced trauma or wishes to understand it more.

This book falls naturally into parts. I begin with the myth of the story in my family as I thought it to be and my perception of the impact it had on the different members of my family.

I then look for the real facts of the story for the first time, to show how stories can get altered and twisted, it can be very hard to step over a boundary of secrecy that has been there for a long time. To prevent the story I tell at the start of the book being influenced by the new information, I wrote the first part of the book before investigating the true story, so the truth really was a surprise to me, a real awakening and you experience that awakening with me.

I go on to examine the idea of generational trauma, epigenetics and the mind body connection to see how trauma may affect people, then I look at some therapeutic ideas to help, so you share my journey. The ideas presented can, I believe, be adapted to cover all kinds, and depths, of family trauma.

Zetta Thomelin - June 2023

Part One

The Story

Chapter one

THE PHOTOGRAPH

The photograph was always there by my grandmother's bed.

It was a black and white photo of a woman in her late twenties with dark waved hair, dark brown eyes and an - almost - smile upon her lips as she clutches a baby in her arms. She looks happy and proud.

I suppose it speaks of the self-absorbed nature of a child that I never asked about the picture. At some point I knew the woman was my aunt and the baby her child, but I did not have an aunt on my father's side, so I did not ask any questions about her, at least not then. When my grandmother died, the picture was moved to my father's bedside and there it stayed until he died, then my mother moved it to the lounge where it sits now. I looked at it this evening, marvelling at how I never asked about my missing aunt and the child in her arms.

I still do not remember when I was told or how. Yes, I know you might think it would be impossible to forget such a thing. When did they decide it was time to tell me? When they thought I would be old enough to understand? Were they worried I would judge her? She was head girl at her school. My grandmother died when I was seventeen, and I thought, even though I knew this was not true, that I was her only grandchild. There had been three grandchildren before I was even born, you see. I knew the story by then, but still did not think this story was real, though the picture was always there and still is now, of the woman with the baby in her arms.

It all happened before I was born, as I say, and nobody was allowed to talk about it, but it cast a shadow over my whole life and still does. I wonder if the shadow would be there without the picture. You know I think it would. After all, there is nothing like the taboo, the unspoken to grow and to thrive in the depths of your mind. Did it make them ill? Dad, grandma, how did they suffer? I do not know as we were never allowed to talk about it. Is it making me ill? Can you pass trauma down the generations? Transgenerational trauma. As a therapist I know this to be true, but it is so hard to apply all the theories to one's own life, one's family that gets tucked out of sight.

My grandmother's head shook all the time, just a little in the early days and then a little more. No-one named it to me, her head just shook, and the teacup would rattle in her hands. After a while her eyes begun to blink rapidly too. I did not think

8

about what this meant, it was just what grandma did.

She was warm and soft and always gave me time, sometimes with her eyes closed when the movement was very bad. She was always smart and correct, an Edwardian through and through, she wore a hat and gloves whenever she left the house.

She kept her dignity no matter how much she shook.

I need to remember that, hold onto that. She lived in a convent and prayed every day, her rosary beads moving through her hands, lips moving too, whispering away. I never thought about the passion in those prayers, the determination in those prayers. Were the prayers for herself, dad, for me to keep the last ones left alive safe. Maybe they were for her daughter, her other grandchildren, her husband, who had all died long before I was born.

I would go and visit grandma once a week. The convent was a large house set in its own grounds with a gravel drive. I would crunch up the drive, then climb up a flight of steps and ring the bell.

A black-clad nun would answer and usher me in. I did not question the unusual setting for a grandma visit, it was just the norm to me, up another flight of steps, past a niche with a statue of the Virgin Mary tucked in and I was at her door. We would start with a chat, well me, twittering away about my week, full of innocent enthusiasm for my latest passions, whether they be a pop star or a book or the drawings I loved doing, she would listen with focused interest, always all her attention. Then we would pore over picture books or maps together, talking about the wider world, she would share her knowledge with me so patiently, then it would be time for tea.

Grandmother was very precise in her requirements, only Tiptree jam would do for the scones with unsalted French butter and Jacob's fruit biscuits on the side. Proper tea in a teapot, with a strainer, no teabags here. Sometimes we would have it in her room, sometimes we would go out and the beige hat and gloves would go on, even in the height of summer. She was rather like an old dowager duchess, four feet nine inches height and fragile like a baby bird, she had a gravitas that could terrorise a waitress at one hundred paces, yet she was so very soft with me.

I have a favourite picture of me with my grandma, we are sitting on the sofa, with me cuddling her, with me smiling, certain in my safety, certain in my love, captured in that moment by the camera. I have searched and searched for this picture, but it has been lost along the way, just preserved in my mind's eye, long may I keep it there.

She lived to the ripe old age of ninety, despite the nodding and the shaking, a fragile heart too.

It is quite commonplace to live so long these

days. She was born in 1892. She lived through the First World War, was a married woman in the Roaring Twenties, having her first child in 1921, another war, all safely pulled through, to lose almost all a decade later.

I always felt my grandmother had an incredible strength to keep going for my father as he had lost so much, she kept going for him as long as she could. Then one morning she sat in her chair by the bed, had a cup of tea and read *The Daily Telegraph*, she read the paper from cover to cover every day. It was found lying on her lap, her heart had just stopped.

I remember the moment when the phone rang. Mum picked up the receiver, we were sitting in the lounge, I could tell something was wrong, but I cannot remember the words, just that moment when she turned to me after she put the phone down and told me Grandma was dead.

It was my first loss, I really felt it, I ran to my room, and I cried, and I cried. Grandma had given me such a sense of security, so much love. If she felt she had a penance to pay, she could not be faulted for her support of her last grandchild, she gave all she possibly could to me.

She was buried in the robes of a Carmelite Nun; they had been waiting in the wardrobe for years. I hope she found the peace she deserved for the suffering she had, for one bad decision, one miscalculation that brought her so much loss and I think so much illness too.

The funeral was in her old parish, where she had lived with her young family, where my father had gone to school.

The whole church community turned out, you see, they all knew what she had lived through, it was so packed, there were people standing at the back. I wish she had known that respect would be there at her passing, not judgement.

I remember standing at her graveside, my very first funeral and as a close family member being handed the aspergillum with holy water in it to sprinkle upon the grave.

I did not quite know what to do with it, I had not paid attention to what my father had done, I was just staring down at the coffin, trying to imagine my grandma in there.

Instead of making the sign of the cross with it, I waved it around over the grave, sprinkling liberally, then felt such shame as I saw others knew what to do, making a careful sign of the cross. I had got it wrong, my cheeks flamed with the shame of it, feeling I had let her down.

I was always unsettled by the head nodding. If I saw anyone doing it, I felt such a surge of pity, I do not want people to pity me.

As a child, although I accepted this was what grandma did, it was still a bit disturbing as it was not talked about, just rather awkwardly ignored. Apparently, I was doing it for quite some time without realising it.

My partner raised it with me once asking if I were aware that I was doing it, I changed the subject. Later, they mentioned again, and I could not believe I could be doing it. Apparently, it happened when I was working on my computer, watching TV, looking at my phone or drifting of in a daze. I asked my mother if she had ever seen my head nodding and she said that yes, she had, but dared not mention it as she did not want to worry me.

The conclusive proof of my tremor came when my partner filmed me nodding away whilst working on my computer. I was behaving just like my grandmother, I was stunned to see it, that thing I had always dreaded was happening to me.

I felt a closeness to her, I wished I had been able to show her understanding of how it felt, the self-consciousness, the new mannerisms of leaning backwards into a chair or resting your hand at the side of the head to try to reduce the movement. I wondered why I had never asked her how she felt when her head shook, or the teacup rattled or about the aunt I never knew.

Was the Parkinson's a taboo subject too? One of the only times I have been really upset about it, was when I wondered if I were to have stepgrandchildren, would they be scared by it? Upset by it? Perhaps it would just be what their strange English grandma did.

I know you probably want to know about the picture, the trauma, but I am not quite ready to get into that yet, I promise I will. I hesitate, because whenever I tell this story, which I have to say is rarely, I see the discomfort of the listener, their judgement and sometimes even a little fear.

I only mention this story because when I was old enough to know, I thought that was why grandma did the nodding and the shaking and when Dad began the shaking too, it is the picture again I thought, that aunt I never knew, who creates all the sadness and the worry and the fear, fear about how it will affect me. Did I become scared and upset by it too?

So, with Dad it started with his right hand shaking and then the left joined in, then the tremors in the leg muscles and his voice began to wane. The night terrors kicked in. When you wake in the night, you struggle to know what is real and what is not, that is how it is for me, and it happened to him so often too.

Sometimes, I dread the night because I hate that confusion of trying to work out what is real and what is not. Maybe this happened to Grandma, another of those questions I did not ask, so many questions.

So many things I would like to ask them about now, how was it for them? I follow reluctantly, hesitantly, oh so hesitantly in their footsteps. But they are not here to ask anymore, nor to ask about the woman in the photograph, in fact no one is left alive who can tell me for real what she was like. I have wondered about checking the newspaper reports but of course it will all be bad, reports of the inquest too. I wonder if you can access inquest information after so many years.

About fifteen years ago I asked my father the exact date of his sister's death.

I had already wanted to know more about this story, but he immediately grasped I was researching it and he began to cry; he was so upset I would have agreed anything to appease him.

He said he did not want me to look for the inquest reports, he did not want me to judge her. He did not, in fact, want me to write about him at all. It was as if he was trying to preserve an image of his sister before it happened, but I had no image of her at all, not good, not bad, by hiding it away, it was all hidden.

In May 2023 it is five years since he died. I am not sure I can be held to that promise now, as my need to know the truth grows, it is a part of my story too, I feel my health nd indeed sanity depends upon me knowing the truth. I wonder if it was a fair promise to extract from me, to keep so much hidden, skulking in the dark.

Chapter two

THE BEGINNING OF THE JOURNEY OF DISCOVERY

The first thing I did to try to understand the story was find out where their graves were, my aunt and her three children, my cousins.

I knew the cemetery, my mother could tell me that, so I approached the local authority, and they sent me a map, I looked at it for a long time. I still have it. They were not buried in Essex where they had lived, but at the cemetery near my grandparents' home, curious. That plot was unvisited for decades. My father never went - to my knowledge - after the funeral and Grandma could not get there without him, though no doubt she was there in her prayers. Hour after hour, those rosary beads, thumbing through her fingers.

Should I go? What would it be like to go?

But I had to go, as this story was haunting me even before I knew that I would be nodding and shaking too. Whilst my father was alive it seemed impossible to go and find them, my missing family, he would just get so upset if I asked anything at all, so it would have felt like a betrayal of him, but now, now I had to do this for me.

A friend said to me when my father died, 'Zetta don't pick up the mantle of their suffering, don't take it from your father and carry it on.' But I knew by now it was too late to stop and that I no longer had any choice but to go.

So, I went to the cemetery clutching my map, walking up and down, row after row, until there it was, a headstone with their names on.

I noticed the children first, Keith, Graham and Carol.

The lettering wasn't etched into the stone but gilded on, most of the gilding had fallen off showing dark patches where the letters had been. There was a large oblong stone surround which was lying broken at one corner, long neglected, all the stone bleached with age. It looked like no one had been there for years, it looked so forlorn, I wondered if their father had ever visited, or whether they were abandoned by everyone.

Seeing the grave made this story somehow more real, they really had existed, this missing part of my family. This missing part that came into the world before me and left before I had a chance to meet them, my generation, my cousins, never to know them.

I sat back on my heels and looked at the names, my aunt too, there she was, in there, down there, the pretty woman from the picture, so alive with that almost smile on her face. Then I cried and I cried for what happened to them and how it hurt and rippled out into the family and all the way down to me. I wept for myself, for the family I would never have, cousins to play with, to get to know as adults, to become friends with, to meet their children, all gone, gone, never to be.

I forgot to take some flowers; how could I forget to take some flowers? It was the least they deserved after so many years of neglect. I roamed around the cemetery in the hope of finding somewhere I could buy some, but no, nothing there, just hundreds of graves and me, not a soul in sight on a grey winter's day.

How could I have forgotten to take the flowers? I would come back, I said, as if I were speaking to them, I will bring some flowers and get the corner of that grave repaired.

I have not been back yet, I tell myself it is a long way to go, I should go back, I tell myself, I really should.

Perhaps when the story is complete, that is the time to return.

When I pulled myself together from my quest for the flowers and appearing like a mad woman crying at a grave from decades ago, I went in search of my grandparents, strangely harder to find. They were in a different part of the cemetery, because of what happened my aunt could not be buried in the Roman Catholic part, this must have really hurt my grandmother. The Catholic part did not have headstones as such, just small rectangular plaques of stone set flat into the grass. I trailed up and down clutching my piece of paper with the number of the grave which in the end was the only way I could identify it, as the grass had grown over most of the wording, virtually obliterated by nature's steady encroachment.

It had been thirty-seven years since I had stood at this spot, at my first encounter with grief and made a fool of myself with my hesitant handling of the aspergillum, how far away that young girl seemed.

I recognised nothing of the place, and I realised as I peered at the fragment of stone I could see, that I had not considered all those years ago that my grandfather was down there too and they would be together at last in their shared grief, so many things I had not considered, thought about or questioned. What a safe place youth seems in a way, no questions, just acceptance of whatever comes your way. My father had clearly not been there for years.

Hiding from the reality of the grief and the loss, I had joined him in that hiding and perhaps am in it still, as I vowed to go back with a trowel and clear it up so you could at least see their names. I felt faintly ashamed of that abandoned grave, but they are never abandoned in my thoughts.

I did not tell my mother I was going to the graves, as I was not sure of how she would react, as she had been caught up in the silence, the taboo for so long too.

When I got home, I found I could not keep quiet about it, it was too moving, too powerful an experience for me to keep it from her, so I rather sheepishly confessed what I had done.

Her response was totally unexpected, she said she wished I had told her, that she would like to have gone too, as she had never been either. I showed her the rather tragic photos I had taken of the deserted graves, and we vowed to arrange to get them tidied up, but quickly we hid again, turned our backs again as it still seemed too hard to hold onto.

Today, I went to Lorenzkirche, a church in the centre of Nuremberg, which I go to on each of my visits to Germany. I always light a candle there for father, Grandma, my uncle Michael, and cousin Zoe, it is a place they never saw but I know they would have loved.

The ceiling is high and vaulted, gothic in style, it looks like a cathedral from centuries gone, triptych gold painted images, statues in blues and golds and reds, the three wise men, the annunciation in a circlet of finely wrought flowers, a giant gold cross with Christ hanging there suspended from the ceiling, suspended there for eons of time, a painting of Saint Sebastian pierced with arrows and the bows in front of him still drawn, stained glass windows in those vibrant colours and St Lawrence is there with his quill in his hand, his robes the purple and the gold and then the humble craftsman Adam crouches by the tabernacle, carved in stone his mason's tool in hand.

I feel I should say here that I am not a practicing Roman Catholic, though my youth was clearly steeped in the religion. I am not unmoved by it, I respect the beliefs of others and feel some comfort in the rituals and so I share them, intertwine them within my own spiritual philosophy and so I sit by the rows of flickering candles and do my remembrance in this focused time in this quiet space.

For the first time, for the very first time, as I sat in this beautiful church in front of the glimmering candles, I thought of my aunt and her children too.

I cannot believe in all this time I had never thought of them in these regular connections with those I have loved and that have gone before me. It felt an intensely important moment, they were becoming more real to me, it seemed that through my writing I was finally giving them a space to be within me.

As I sat, a woman came to light a candle too and she crossed herself then sank down upon her knees and she sobbed and sobbed, muttering some prayers in between her gulps for air. I felt her grief wash out of her and swirl around me, I wondered about her story, her loss, as I gritted my teeth in an effort not to be swept away by it, our griefs intertwining and swirling around the pews and up the aisles.

This journey into the past started with the head nodding and the movement in the muscles of my legs, because it connected me so strongly with my father and grandmother.

One day, I was resting my legs up on a chair and I noticed a twitching in the muscles of my calf, goodness I thought, that looks just like what Dad's legs did, must be a one off, it just cannot be, not me too, surely not me too, then of course the head nodding could be ignored no longer and the twitching spread, sometimes my foot, sometimes my thighs, then there were the terrors in the night.

That trauma has nothing to do with me, I had always felt that is what caused the nodding and the shaking for them, it had to be, surely.

I thought I thought, it will help with the healing, it feels necessary now somehow, to let it out, give it some space to breathe, then maybe it will not need to attack my body as it attacked theirs. So let me tell you the whole story, the story as I know it to be.

Chapter three

Let me please start by setting the scene.

My grandfather was a Frenchman, a commandant in the *Armée de l'Air*, based in London during the Second World War, working with General De Gaulle recruiting special agents to be dropped into the field of operations in France for the Free French.

When Pétain capitulated to Hitler, many Frenchmen felt he should have fought on and those who could get away came to London, joined the British forces, or worked with the Free French to maintain a resistance movement on the ground in France.

My grandfather was extremely proud to be working with De Gaulle and was lucky enough to have his family with him. His son, my father was a boy still at school, his daughter, my aunt, was a young woman by then having been a bright girl at school and yes, ending up as Head Girl, she was popular with everyone who met her. The family was comfortable, middle class, my grandmother

23

never cooked a meal in her life, she could perhaps just boil an egg at a push, she had someone to do all that for her and to take care of the house, not an opulent life but certainly a good one.

After the war my grandfather, awarded the Legion d'Honneur, was offered the Governorship of Tahiti by the French Government, seen as a reward for his services to France, but his family was settled in London, so instead he worked for French Aerospace and a French Bank based in London. The bank had operated throughout the war but separately and it needed to be integrated back into the main business in France which my grandfather was tasked with, my father when he left school followed his father into the same bank.

My aunt was introduced to various young French officers and pilots in the early 1940s by her parents, with the hope of a marriage, but she seemed to want to rebel against her suburban middle-class life and perhaps also the sense of difference which the strong French influence brought into her life.

From the modern perspective one may not be aware of how much anti-French feeling there was in Britain during the Second World War. Due to the capitulation of France to Hitler, the relationship between the Free French and British forces was an uneasy one, the mood of the public who felt deserted in their fight against Hitler was even worse.

I was told a story of my grandfather walking down the street in London in his French uniform being spat at and called a coward, this must have been very galling for him. So, my aunt I think wanted to feel more British, during the war she did her bit by joining the Women's Air Force which she seemed to enjoy and then one fateful night in a London air raid shelter she met the man she was to go on to marry.

We can only speculate how differently the story for all of us would have been, were it not for that meeting. He was a corporal in the British army from Essex and had a very different life experience to my aunt, she found it exciting and different and so the die was cast. She went to live in very straightened circumstances in Essex and being, indeed, a good Catholic girl, the babies came. She was constantly struggling to have enough money to feed the children, I still have letters from her to my father asking for help. He gave her as much as he could each month, but he was a young married man himself by then too and had his own responsibilities.

We can never know what went on in that marriage behind closed doors and to conjecture would be unfair to them both. I do not want, by setting the scene of the story, to appear to be making excuses for what she did, but I am a therapist, and my job is to understand why people do the things that they do, and all our actions have meaning however distorted that meaning may be. However, something was not right in the marriage.

Near the end of her life, she approached my grandmother for help and asked if she and the three children could come and live with her, she was pregnant yet again.

My grandmother said, no, which would turn out to be the worst decision of her life. We need to look at the context again here, it was by now the 1950s, you were expected to make the best of a marriage. She had broken away from her family to some extent with this marriage and I fear to say there may have been a degree of 'you have made your bed now lie in it.' We also must take into account the family's staunch Catholicism, there could be no divorce, it would not be countenanced.

Saying no to this request would have undoubtedly haunted my grandmother every day for the rest of her life. I cannot begin to imagine how deeply this must have cut her, how wrong she was, how she did not grasp what my aunt must have been going through to make such a drastic appeal. In fact, I have letters written not long after my grandmother's own marriage   home to her mother. She had moved far away from her family as my grandfather set up an aeroplane company in northern France after the First World War. In the letters she said she was not happy with married life, her own mother told her to get on with it, it is what women had to do.

Grandma loved her husband, over the years this is certainly clear, though at first, she entered marriage as an idealistic, over protected young woman and had not reckoned on the realities of married life, the ups, and the downs. When she got the same letter from her own daughter, she would have compared it to her own very different situation and felt it would come good in the end for her too.

How very wrong she was to pass that advice down another generation. She learned a very hard lesson and I know she learned it, as not long before she died, she took me to one side and said 'Darling, I feel that you are not the marrying kind, do not let society force you into a life that is not right for you, be yourself.'

These are important words that I have carried with me over the years as I battled against conformity, and though I am now married, it is a marriage of a very different kind. I wonder if that is what she saw, so much more that I could have given her credit for at the time, as I tried to hide myself away from the light for fear that anyone would see in those fragile teenage years.

You may notice that I do not use my aunt's name anywhere, I am reticent to do so as she was so pilloried by the press after her death. I feel I would be joining the ghoulish spectators for focusing too much upon her. I feel she needs privacy now after all these years, the focus of this story is the aftermath of one person's actions within a family, that can ripple through the generations. I want to leave her in essence to any peace that I hope she may have found.

So, I must say it, what she did, you may have guessed by now.

One April day she took a pillow and smothered her three children and then put her head in the gas oven, they all died. There you have it, the blight of my family.

What she did was of course monstrous, but I cannot see her as a monster, as no doubt she was depicted in the press. I have not dared to look at that yet. She was by all reports a loving mother and the pictures I have seen of Keith, Graham and Carol are of three happy boisterous children.

One can only begin to imagine, as she reached a point of despair, that she could not live this life anymore that it felt better for her children to accompany her wherever she thought that would be, than to leave them behind with their father, maybe she felt that she could not be parted from them or was it what she would be leaving them to?

The story continues like this, that my father was out of the country, I can only imagine away on business for the bank. When he returned, he was at the airport and he bought a newspaper, I have it in my mind that it was *The Daily Mirror* that had the biggest headline that had caught his attention, the headline about this child killer, his sister the child

28

killer blazoned across the front page, the first he was to know about it.

I have no idea if this part of the story is a myth, I have no idea when I picked it up, but it sits in my mind. Can you imagine what he felt? I think about the relationship he must have had with those children, perhaps playing football in the garden with Graham and Keith, or perhaps Carol sat on his knee whilst he read her a bedtime story.

I know he loved them, wanted to protect them, and felt he had failed them. His big sister too, he looked up to her, he felt he was never quite as bright as her, as sparkling as her and see how it ended, an utter tragedy.

When he got to his parents' house, the press was camped outside, wanting to see the family that bred this child killer, as I write, I can again not begin to imagine that fragile grandmother I loved so much, so little and frail trying to support the weight of her grief and keep her men safe in this spotlight of reviling condemning as she processed her loss.

I did not get to meet my grandfather, that war hero of two wars, pilot in the first, won the Croix de Guerre six times, very rare, a man of courage and integrity that I know my father always felt he could not live up to. He was broken by the grief, one battle he just could not win. He died at sixty-nine, ostensibly of pneumonia, but I think it was of a broken heart and perhaps, just perhaps, if not for that meeting in the air raid shelter, he would have lived, I would have known him, how I wish I had known him, one of the many losses from that critical April day.

Chapter four

THE AFTER-EFFECT

MY GRANDMOTHER

I have already said much about my grandmother and her life, but it would not be complete without saying a little more. She lived with us for some years after my grandfather's death, until she went into the convent when I was eleven. She immersed herself in her faith, when many would have been driven away from God for allowing such a tragedy to happen, for her, it was her comfort.

Along with her personal prayers, she said the daily prayers of a Carmelite nun each day and attended Mass every day until the day she died, despite all her love and care and closeness to me.

I never once saw her smile, not once, in those seventeen years, nor did I hear her laugh, something I had not realised until the reflection brought on by this writing. A pall of sadness hung around her neck, which even a self-absorbed child could not entirely miss.

The photograph, it was always there, always a reminder, just the one, the one with the almost smile on her lips, taken at the beginning of her married life, Keith the eldest, the first grandchild clasped in a loving mother's arms.

MY FATHER

And my father, what happened to him?

My father, despite the wreckage of his family life, did smile, in fact when I remember him from childhood, he seemed to always be smiling at me, he dealt with things in a very different way.

He became a playboy, a party animal, living for the moment, I think he felt that life was so harsh he was going to squeeze every bit of fun he could out of it, parties on yachts in the south of France, thanks to those rich clients at the bank, parties, parties, parties.

He was somewhat reckless, lost his pious faith, railed at God for a while. He left his first wife and found my mum, but more of that anon. They had fun together, partied together and then I came along. I was loved by him, almost too much. I think of those nephews and niece who came before me and how I was treasured, kept close and protected with almost a fierce fear.

They still had the parties after I was born, an early memory he used to recount of me, was overseeing putting me to bed one night, his turn, they had people coming round, I would not settle down, every time he went to leave me, I would jump up wide awake again, wail and protest.

After several false starts at departure he thought the moment of escape had come, but to be sure, he got down on all fours and crawled slowly and quietly across to the door to create the very least sound, when he stood up to open the door, he turned round, looking over his shoulder to check I was still asleep and there I was standing up in my cot looking at him curiously at this strange behaviour. At this point he gave up, no doubt laughing and took me into the party and danced around and around with me!

So, he danced, and he partied his way away from the memories, he hid from it, he would not talk about it. It was as if it did not happen. Real denial. He would laugh, he would joke and play the fool, with a fierce grasping at life, a pushing and daring at life to stop him from taking all he could from it.

As part of my father's rebellion against life and what was expected of him, came one wonderful action, well wonderful for me. The bank he worked for wanted to transfer him up to Glasgow to set up a new branch or to set up a new branch somewhere in France, he had been instrumental in establishing their South Kensington office and they saw it as his forte. This led him to a big life change, he resigned from the bank, threw away the stability and the pension, grew his hair long, donned a pair of jeans and decamped to Cornwall where the good life beckoned. I used to call him 'old man hippy.' He was only in his thirties!

My grandmother was not thrilled, saying he looked like a French railway operative, not quite what she expected of her son, though in time she saw that he was at last happy, so she adapted to the new life he created for us all. Anything to keep him happy. She would never say no to a child again, she had learned the folly of that. Though it was her home he sold to pay the way for that change, taking her away from all she knew, for the new life that beckoned.

My parents bought a big square house on the side of a valley, on a piece of land that swept down to a river, wild untamed land which was a place of magical adventure for an inquisitive, imaginative child. I fought my way through the undergrowth, out of a little gate at the end of the garden and was in moments by a cascading waterfall, gallons of water surging down through a hole in a rock, thundering, pounding down, day and night, the sound accompanied all that we did, and I found it both exhilarating and comforting. Merlin the magician's cave was supposed to be hidden behind the waterfall, my world became full of made-up stories of spells and of knights following their quests, as I galloped around on my imaginary steed.

My parents bought a shop in the nearby village of Tintagel. There, they began a completely new life, mixing with other London dropouts, models and dancers and the Foot's Barn players, an acting troop that fussed over me, dressed me up and covered me in greasepaint. It was a happy time for me and an escape from the past for my parents, I think my father found some peace there in Cornwall.

I don't think my father would have dropped out and broken away from all that was expected of him, if it were not for the tragedy, he was questing for an antidote to the pain and he found it in the wild untamed land of the west and the rebels that congregated there.

This is the one and only positive I can see to what happened, for me it meant a freedom too, I roamed as a child wherever I wanted to go, made great friends, I lived a real and free life which gave me a love of the land that I have carried with me, which has sustained me through life's trials and tribulations. Cornwall has been for me, my sanctuary, a place of magic and wonder, of happy memories almost outside of time, always there to retreat to.

It was a utopia not to last, the financial crisis of the 1970s bit hard on the tourist industry, affecting our businesses and in the end, we returned to London when I was eleven, a terrible move for me. I loathed the constraint of city life, and I could not understand why my parents had uprooted it me and taken me there.

My father worked for a French company in London, his hair was cut short again and the jeans exchanged for a suit. He seemed to be happy enough despite the change. I think it was good to have some French people around him. We settled down and all was quiet for a while as the years in Cornwall had affected their cure.

May father was twenty-six when my aunt died and he tried to escape from his memories and feelings, but it would not all stay at bay forever. When he was in his fifties, one night, my mother and he sat down in front of the TV for the usual evening's entertainment, they had not looked at any programme guide. A drama was on, which they decided to watch. As the story unfolded it was about a pregnant woman, with three children, whom she killed and then killed herself, there seems no doubt it was an adaptation of my aunt's story, with no consultation with the family or thought of those left still living with this tragedy.

My lovely laughing, smiling, loving, fun dad, snapped, broke open, it all came flooding back. I was telling a friend this story and she said she had seen the same programme, had no doubt it was not accidental, just close to the truth, she felt it was the story of my aunt, out there on TV for everyone to see. My aunt who murdered her own children and then put an end to herself.

He changed then, my dad, I struggled to recognise him at first. He turned back to the church, having rejected it totally in his twenties. He became very devout, he picked up the mantle of those daily prayers, the rosary beads now passing through his fingers. The Roman Catholic church had changed a great deal in the years he had been gone, no more sung Latin mass and confession had been repackaged into reconciliation, but he was stuck in a much harsher 1950s church. He was constantly in search of forgiveness for not saving his sister, nephews, and niece, expecting a level of maturity unlikely in his younger self, a young man of twenty-six, with his own life to live.

A family priest once said to my dad, you have been shriven, you are forgiven, your sin lies in not accepting that forgiveness.

Still, he was bowed down with the burden of the guilt and the grief, on bended knee, still begging for forgiveness right up to the very end. He was a good and loving, caring man and it really broke my heart to see this burden he carried, which no one could relieve from him. I sometimes feel angry at her, my aunt, for taking away my family, that family I never had and for hurting my father and grandmother so much, but it passes, fizzles out, burns out in the end and I am left with an ache and pity for it all.

One day, when he was in his seventies, he went

to a reunion of people he had been at school with in London during the war. One man came up to him and introduced himself and then said, 'You are the man whose sister killed her children, aren't you?' It is hard to imagine someone being that insensitive. It absolutely shattered him, he was so upset, even at seventy he could not outrun the infamy of the story, his family tainted forever, the sister he loved clearly so much, remembered as the child killer. I think that is why he asked me not to research the story, as he did not want me to judge her, to know her for her one terrible deed and not all those years before, of the woman she had been, the loving big sister to him, he did not want one moment of madness to blight her memory forever.

As he would not talk of my aunt, what do I know of her, but the stories and reports often by those who never knew her.

So deep was the feeling of responsibility that he had for his big sister, that when the doctors were experimenting with his Parkinson's medication, it brought on hallucinations and confusion, it became so bad that we had to call the paramedics and he told them that he had killed his sister. They took me aside and asked what kind of a man he had been and could he have hurt his sister. I was so upset, he was the softest, most gentle man and I tried to explain he meant by not saving her, he had been responsible for her death.

It was a terrible time, he was truly tormented.

Until they got the medication right, it seemed to
release all his demons, all the suppressed horror, it
came out all over again. So, I watched him suffer
over the years for this event so far back in the past,
before I was born, still blighting my life in a
different decade, a different century and it hurts me
still, as I feel my head nodding, my muscles
moving, I cannot help but feel a link in the chain
of suffering.

MY UNCLE

There is someone who cannot go unmentioned in
this story and that is the husband of my aunt, it is
only as I write this, I realise he is/was my uncle,
the uncle I never met. He lost his whole family one
cold April day. Did he find them, I wonder? Did he
walk through the door after a day at work
expecting to be greeted by the hustle and bustle of
family life to be greeted by silence, a deadly
silence? Where did he go first? Bounding upstairs
to check on the children's rooms or into the kitchen
to see why he could not smell his supper cooking
only to find his wife there, lying dead instead.

Did he fear at first when he heard the silence as
he opened the front door that his wife and the
children had left him, only to be greeted by a far
worse outcome? Did he wish it had only been that
afterwards? What a total horror if it were he, that
walked through that door first. Or was it a

neighbour who found them or a friend popping round for a chat? I do not yet know, but a tragedy from which he too would never truly recover, how could he? Nor any person who walked into that cold, dead house and found the nightmare in there.

He is one of the main victims of this story. I have it in mind that he did remarry, well that was the family myth, though I have not researched this yet. Perhaps he had children in this second marriage, they might even read this story. Were they told of what had happened to their father before they came along, if indeed they exist?

It was strange enough to discover I was not the one and only treasured grandchild and that others had trod that path before me, so how would it be to find your father had three dead children in the past and that they were your half-siblings? Maybe it was another secret to be stashed away. If they do know, I have wondered about these imaginary children if it has affected their lives too. They probably would not exist at all if it had not been for that desperate act by my aunt, what a conundrum!

Could there be others around complicit in this story? A neighbour who did not want to get involved or a hesitant friend? Did they lie awake at night after the revelation and curse themselves for not acting, just as my family cursed themselves for not noticing, not seeing how desperate things had become, for being blind to the tragedy about to unfold in front of them?

We seem to have this almost innate learning not to get involved in other people's lives, particularly in English society, not to interfere in the goings-on behind closed doors. I wonder if some catastrophic events could be avoided if we showed a little more care and did not look the other way, passing the buck to some other source, an unknown other who can make everything right.

There can be no doubt that my aunt must have suffered from depression, you would have to be in an extreme crisis mentally to do such a terrible thing and there were very limited support systems then for mental health and certainly there would have been no-one for her husband to turn to for help as there would be today.

I cannot help but wonder what kind of a man my uncle was, though he could never imagine the outcome of any words he may have said, any more than my grandmother could. If in any way he contributed to the events that happened, he has paid a heavy price for it. It may sound like there is some judgement of him, perhaps seeing him in some way at fault, this was I think picked up from my family, an undercurrent of judgement which I am struggling to shake off. Maybe it was a survival tactic to give him some of the blame to deflect from their own shame. I am telling this story from the scraps of information, the insinuations that I have picked up over the years where I could, we may find more truth as the quest evolves.

Whatever the circumstances, whether he was a good man or a difficult man, he suffered a horrendous loss. I am sure he must be dead now too as all the main protagonists in this story are, though his children, if there are children, would be about my age now. I say again, I make no judgement on your father, he is a man I never knew, all I can ever do is wonder what happened in her and in that family to lead to such a drastic act.

MY YOUNGER SELF

I need to acknowledge how this story might have affected me when I was a teenager, as I think it did. I suffered from anxiety, many teenagers do, about the usual things particularly not fitting in, not being pretty enough, clever enough.

Then one day I had my first panic attack when I was sitting with my parents watching a television programme. It was a rather graphic dramatization about the ancient Greek, Ptolemy, there was a scene that I can still see in my mind's eye now, in which someone had their eyes gouged out. This seemed quite violent and realistic for a BBC2 play of the day.

Within seconds I was having my first panic attack. It was quite severe, I was gasping for breath, hyperventilating until my limbs began to tingle and go numb. My parents did not know what was happening and called a doctor. When I was assured that I was not dying, which is a feeling anyone who has had a panic attack will have known, I began to calm down, my breathing slowing, the tingling easing.

This first panic attack started a phase of more extreme social anxiety that went on through my teens. I had little support from my GP who just gave me Valium, which I flushed down the toilet as I wanted to resolve things for myself. So, I read books about anxiety as there was no offer of counselling or other talking therapies at that time. This is where the effect of the tragedy comes in.

My parents became deeply worried by my anxiety, I could sense their fear, you could taste and smell their fear that I was in some way going to end up like my aunt. That is how I interpreted their worry, that I was mentally ill and unable to cope. I knew about the story by then and I found it so very troubling to feel their fear.

Of course, I can understand why they would be concerned, as an adult looking back on their situation, but then I did not really understand it or that it probably had nothing to do with fear connected to my aunt.

I have never ever had a suicidal thought in my life, I have not had depression, low mood from time to time due to a life situation, but I am very positive and feel very strong. I had some anxiety as a teenager, all those hormones raging, and I think in my case I was still struggling from the transition from Cornish idyll to a London life.

But I wondered at the time, if they knew something about me that I did not, I began to worry that I might do something to hurt myself without realising it, I read the fear in my father's face, in his every word and my worry increased.

Maybe I might kill myself in my sleep I thought, could that be possible? I read avidly anything I could find about sleep walking, it seems you will not do anything in your sleep that you would not do in real life, this comforted me for a while. Then I reasoned, what if I were having a dream in which something so terrible was going to happen to me it would be my only recourse, if I acted out this dream, I might kill myself without meaning to! And so, the worry increased. Maybe it is in my genes I thought, maybe I cannot escape it.

The worry grew so huge that I began to hide things at night that could be a danger to me, like knives and bottles of bleach. My adolescent self did not seem to realise that I would know where I had put them, my subconscious was far from daft, but still the only way I would allow myself to sleep, was when everything was safely stowed away. I eventually abandoned this nocturnal routine after reading about a man who would tie himself to the bed to stop himself sleep walking only to discover his sleep walking self was quite capable of untying a knot!

The years from sixteen to eighteen were difficult, my school which I loved only went up to sixteen, I was going to go elsewhere for my A levels, but in the end, I studied from home and became more and more withdrawn and reclusive. My parents worried even more. I feel that if my father had not been so secretive about the family tragedy and we could have had an open conversation about it, I could have dispelled any misapprehensions and I would not have been hiding bottles of bleach in the night. We are so sensitive to mood at that age, watching every adult's response to us, to gauge our place in the world and of course we see ourselves at the centre of it.

Everything changed for me in a rather unusual way. I followed a pop star very avidly, listening to music hour upon hour in my room. She was performing in London in a play, having not left the house for months, my parents encouraged me to go and see it. They bought me a ticket and dropped me off outside the theatre where a friend was waiting for me and urged me quickly towards the stage door where she was signing autographs. When we got there, I shyly hung back, my idol came over to me, she started talking to me, shone her attention upon me and I began to come out of my shell. She suggested I come to the show again which I did, I made new friends with a lot of her fans, became a part of a group, and felt I belonged somewhere at last.

A new life for me began, after this meeting, I left my anxiety in the past, became gradually more outgoing and was then set to head off for university. Life became fun at last. The worry began to leave my parents' faces, the relief was palpable, though they were not keen when I started staying out all night rather than holing up in my room, but at last I had proved I had outrun my genes. Or so I thought until the head nodding and the muscle trembling began.

There was one other impact upon my life which I initially saw as rather benign, but in fact it affected the whole family dynamic. I was very close to my father, I have already stressed the focus and the care lavished upon me, but it was also very intense, it was all that I knew so I did not see it as anything other than what any family would be like.

When I left home my father and I would write letters to each other, at one point they were in French, and I loved this special connection to him. He would also write great essays for me to read about things that interested us, sometimes in letter form.

There was a period in my life when after an illness my sight was affected, and he recorded tapes for me then to maintain this connection. Many of this I have kept, it all sits in a box beneath my bed, it has been there untouched since his death five years ago. I cannot bring myself to look at it

46

yet, it is too painful. I want to make very clear there was nothing untoward in this intensity, it was emotional and intellectual.

I always saw myself as lucky to have this great relationship with my father, it was only when my partner said that I saw him as perfect and that it was very hard for anyone to compete with his position in my heart, that I began to wonder about how this might have affected my mother.

I wondered if she felt a little on the outside of the triangle and I wish I had understood this when my father was still alive. I think it may have created a strain between the three of us, my mother may have felt she never quite fitted in.

My grandmother lived with us for a while and was a part of this intense connection with dad too, joined by their suffering, my mother must have felt very much an outsider in her own home sometimes. I have subsequently asked her about this, and she said she did feel sometimes on the outside of this tight group connected by grief and blood ties that she felt she could not break through.

When my father lay dying, following a worsening of his Parkinson's so that he could no longer swallow, my mother and I took turns to sit with him. When it was clear he was in his last moments, we were both there. I took it upon myself to read to him from *The Prophet* by Kahlil Gibran, I wanted him to hear a familiar voice, I hoped it gave him comfort.

It was a book he had given my mother in their early courtship, and I thought it brought us all together. Sometime after his death I asked my mother if she had objected to my reading to him as he lay dying. She said she had found it difficult. I realised I had intruded on the last moments of their life together; I had selfishly wanted my voice to be the last he heard, no doubt it did give him comfort, but I was still trying to assert my pole position in his heart. I know now that I was wrong.

This special relationship I feel came again from that loss of the first children my father had loved, he poured everything from those three into me and I lapped it up, who would not? But I feel maybe it damaged my relationship with my mother and with many previous partnerships too, at least at last I am processing this as part of this journey into the forbidden story.

MY MOTHER

I wonder what it was really like for my mother.

She met my father not that long after it happened. He was married to someone else, but I think his grief and distress had driven his wife away and she was having an affair with a colleague of his at the bank. It is harder to write about my mother as she is still alive and may, just may one day read this, it makes my hand more hesitant across the keys.

My parents met at a gathering of mutual friends in a pub in the Haymarket, my mother was working for Cox and Kings at the time and there seemed to be a crossover between her work and that of the bank.

They clicked straight away and began to meet regularly; it was reported to me that one of the things Dad said very quickly was that he wanted mum to be the mother of his children. This interests me, as the loss of his nephews and niece would still have been very fresh, and there seems a drive here to continue the family, to in a sense replace what was lost, or at least not let this family end with a full stop.

My father was granted a divorce, and my parents were married within a year of meeting, marrying on the very day the decree absolute was issued. They spent the rest of their lives together. I have, since my father died got small fragments of information from my mother about the tragedy. She felt he still carried the distress of his loss when they met. His wife was part of an old life, that involved the part of his family that was gone, with mum he could reinvent his life without a sister and her family, papering over the cracks, he could not do this with someone who had lived through the trauma with him.

My mother struggled with him not talking about it and of course took the brunt of his distress when things all erupted again in his later life. The only scraps of information she ever received, she did not receive from Dad or Grandma, but from his aunt and the rest of the family in France. It was from them she learned that my aunt had been pregnant when she died. Mum wondered if Dad had known this detail or if somehow it had been kept from him.

My father's late return to the church affected their relationship, as a Catholic there could be no divorce, he should not have remarried and this really troubled him, it made me conceived in sin and him having lived in sin with my mother for decades.

When his first wife died this was resolved by my parents marrying in the local Catholic church. So I had the rather odd experience of attending my own parents' wedding, I wondered which side of the church I should stand on. I may sound flippant, but I found the whole thing very difficult, but we all went through with it for him.

I think she let him get his own way in many things, always compensating, adapting to any plans and ideas he had as a form of appeasement for his loss. She has to an extent taken on the mantle of the loss too. My father used to have masses said on the day of the deaths of my aunt and the children and mum carries this on in his stead and of course keeps that picture there. I am wondering what will happen to it when she is gone. Do I put it away at last, will that be possible? I am hoping it will or maybe this writing will be the closure that we all need.

As I finish off consideration of my small triumvirate family, I suddenly realise that I might not exist if this tragedy had not happened, as my father might not have left his wife or been a person who could even leave his wife as he may have stayed an active Catholic, so never mind my uncle's new family might not exist, what about me!

COUSIN JACKIE

My father had a cousin, somewhere between himself and his sister in age, I do not know much about her relationship with my aunt, but she was very close to my father, slipping into the role of surrogate sister of sorts once his sister was gone.

Jackie played a big part in my young life. She was an opera singer, an actress and a model. When I was a child she would sweep into any room with great drama, immediately taking centre stage, she was beautiful, flamboyant, and almost camp. I was mesmerised by her as a child, I hung upon her every word, though she became increasingly eccentric with age. As, with all the family we never spoke about the tragedy, but one day in the later stages of her life, she suddenly talked about it.

I remember the conversation clearly, Jackie had phoned my parent's house, they were out, and so I picked up the phone, I was sitting in my father's study, and she just began to talk. I remember it vividly as it was such a surprise, maybe she felt this was her last chance or an only chance to talk to me about it with no-one else around. She had been in the Women's Air Force like my aunt, but this was after the war. She claimed that not long before her death my aunt had visited her at her base and had poured out her distress and unhappiness she felt in her marriage.

Jackie said that my aunt should never have married and did not understand fully at the time what it would mean for her as she had been so young. Jackie felt such guilt that she had not done anything to help despite the obvious despair, though she had not realised she was at quite such a breaking point, especially with another baby due.

She complained of her husband's physical attentions and the implication was that she really could not cope with this part of the marriage at all, and Jackie said that my aunt was essentially gay, but had not realised it before her marriage, that she could not connect in a physical way with men.

I have wondered at this as a conversation, as it happened in the 1950s. Would she really have expressed this kind of identification? I feel the cousin put a modern spin on the conversation, of course, we shall never know. It troubled me in many ways hearing this, how trapped she must have felt, how confused, and misunderstood, if only someone had presented to her a way out. Each way she turned she was told to stay put and it would all feel better eventually. It seems she could not wait.

THE FAMILY IN FRANCE

I cannot leave this part of the story without mentioning the family and the house in France. We used to go over to France every year to see the family there, on the Normandy coast, a family of fishermen, harbour masters and clock makers over the generations. My grandfather had wanted to go to sea like his ancestors, but he was colour blind, so he took to the air instead. This may sound surprising from a 21st Century perspective, but when he wanted to become a sailor communication between ships was done by coloured flags and you needed to be able to read these communications accurately, of course now becoming a pilot would be prevented by colour blindness.

The house in France had some land around it on which they grew all sorts of fruit and vegetables, but the most impressive thing there was the wine cellar, even as a child I could see the care with which the wines were chosen and stored, a typical French home!

Aunt Bertilde, my father's aunt, lived there with her son, daughter, and a son in law, still all in the house in those days, they were a little older than my parents.

My father's uncle Paul, after whom he was named, was long dead. I should probably mention here that there was another daughter, cousin to my aunt who was missing from the house, the eldest child, Paulette, she had been sectioned and committed to an asylum in the late 1940s, never to return.

I did not learn of this until I reached my adulthood, another hidden story and perhaps why the French family felt such a kinship over what happened with my aunt. There must be some genetic weakness there which thankfully is one that has bypassed me. I will settle for the shaking and the nodding if it means I miss out on the depression! There have been no grandchildren there in France, so I am the last from that family, it all stops with me.

My memories of the house are of sitting around a big kitchen table with a plastic cloth and lots of vibrant talk eddying around me in French, lots of warm smiles, then running around the garden, hoping to steal the pea pods and eat them without being caught. Cousin Jean, in a vest and track suit bottoms standing in the garden, leaning on his spade with a cigarette permanently pressed to his lower lip. My first taste of Calvados at eleven years old was at that kitchen table and left me giggling and giggling for hours, feeling such a grown-up, included, a part of everything.

One thing I did not know until more recent

times was that there was a room in that house set aside as a shrine to my aunt and the children. It was full of pictures of them with the curtains drawn closed, no one was to open them, it was a place of memorial, an acknowledgement that they had lived and died.

Those children, who must have sat at that table too and run around the garden just like me on their summer holidays, then down to the beach to play in the sand and search through the scattered shells for a souvenir to take home.

Aunt Bertilde made such a fuss of me, was so very generous to me, she took me out one day to a jeweller and asked the jeweller to present a tray of gold watches for me to choose from, so exciting it was, I felt like a grown-up. My mother was embarrassed at the cost when she saw them and suggested another tray to choose from, but Bertilde said only the best for me and I chose my watch with great pride, it remained one of my treasures, until sadly it was stolen from me. I did not really compute at the time, that again, those three children had been there before me and the family were hanging on to me for dear life, the last child of that generation that there would ever be.

I think perhaps I felt the strength of emotion there with the family in France, but never truly understood it, the attention I got, the fuss I got. My father's cousins too, would of course have known Keith, Graham and Carol, played with them and had perhaps a story to tell were they allowed, were it not the secret, locked away in the bedroom upstairs.

So, we have a tragic event that affected the main protagonists, my father, grandparents, and my uncle. The cousins and aunt in France. Cousins here. The neighbours. Friends. My mother and I when we became a part of the story. My uncle's new wife must have been affected and any children he had, even if they knew nothing about it, it must have affected their father's relationship with them. One person's act in a moment of distress and the ripples affecting so many. That is just in this story, how many tragedies out there are rippling through communities and tearing them apart, tearing lives apart.

I have left my panic attacks behind long ago, but my physical problems have brought me to this point of trying to find some answers and writing the story is a part of the process to let it see the light after so many years in hiding. I hope too, to spur others to process their stories and not leave them festering in the dark for years.

Chapter five

Family stories are often distorted, as there is so much secrecy. One finds oneself sometimes filling in the gaps, without realising it, and creating a different story. I knew I needed to break my promise to my father and find out the truth, to see how this affected my understanding of my family and my place in it. So here is the truth as much as I could find. We can only deal with the problems within a family by facing them, instead of hiding from them.

Death Certificates

I began my quest by looking for some newspaper headlines for 1956, as this was when I had been told my aunt had died, but I found nothing. I decided to look for her death certificate, perhaps this was a better start point. I found it two years earlier and registered in a different part of Essex from the one that I had believed she lived in.

The most attentive of you will wonder why I did not know the date from visiting the graves. All I can say is that was three years earlier and I seem to have blotted out the dates I saw then. 1956 had stuck with me as the date for many years. Already, at this very first step, there is a discrepancy, so what else might be wrong in my knowledge of this story? I wondered about getting the death certificates for the children, but I was not ready for that yet.

It dawned on me that my father would have only been twenty-four when my aunt died, that seems so young. How could a twenty-four-year-old young man be expected to have foreseen or understood the potential tragedy unfolding in his life, to have saved them all from it, especially at a time when mental health was barely considered at all? Stiff upper lip and don't make a fuss! We had just come out of a terrible war, and everyone was expected to just be grateful to be alive, when there had been so much suffering, fear, and deprivation in the last decade.

As I waited for the death certificate for my aunt to arrive, I began to feel very angry in a new way, that by supressing this story and hiding it away, through guilt or maybe shame, the children had been hidden away too, erased as if they had never been. If three children had been murdered by a stranger, there would be a neatly tended grave with flowers year by year, not the neglected broken tomb that I had found. Their existence had been blotted out and erased and as these children gradually became more and more real to me, not an abstract story to be whispered behind our hands, I wanted justice for them, I wanted them to be acknowledged and known again, so my passion for this quest to find out about them grew.

MY AUNT

I now have my first piece of real data, the death certificate of my aunt. It raises more questions and sheds some light too. My understanding of the way she died is confirmed, 'asphyxia by coal gas poisoning, self-administered, the balance of the deceased mind being at the time disturbed', this statement was following the coroner's report. The occupation of my uncle is listed as that of 'a men's outfitter's manager'. This does not fit with the impression of the wild boy from an underprivileged background who had served as a professional soldier, that had grown-up in the family mythology.

It sounds very respectable, and one would imagine reasonably paid. My image of him begins to shift. I note also as a point of history, that my uncle's occupation is on her death certificate, it is listed under 'Rank or Profession' of the deceased, thus as a housewife and mother, your husband's rank is noted, showing your place in society. Hard to believe that this was still the case in such relatively recent times.

The other interesting factor is the date. We have already ascertained that it was two years earlier than I had thought, but I checked the date to find what day of the week it was and to my surprise it was a Saturday. My image of him coming home from work to find them could indeed still be true if he worked on a Saturday. I wondered what more I would find out. That isolation and loneliness I had conjured in my mind for her, does not sit with a Saturday when other family or friends could have been around to support her. The date of the inquest is on the certificate which will help with the next stage of the quest, which I hope will shed light on the events that day.

The address of the house is on the certificate. I was intrigued as to what their home was like, so I looked for it on google. It is an end-of-terrace property, valued at around £350,000 in the current market, so not a garret by any stretch of the imagination. They may not have owned it, perhaps just renting, but it looks like a nice home in a respectable area. The myth of her squalid existence exploded, perhaps.

Looking at this certificate was the next step to reality from the grave visit. The grave told me they all did exist, it is not a myth, the certificate proves my aunt did take her own life, it is starkly there in black and white.

I have ordered just one of the children's death certificates now, which will be much harder to see. I have chosen the child I believe to be the eldest. I feel I cannot hide from this completely and there may be more information there that could be useful.

KEITH

I now have Keith's death certificate and the first thing I notice is that he is only nine, not eleven as I had thought. My image of him changes a little, I skip across the columns to the cause of death which is a shocker and hard to read: 'Asphyxia by drowning due to murder by .....' So, he was drowned not smothered as the myth had it. This feels somehow more brutal, a more active form of killing, it shakes me and of course I need to know more now, what about the other two children, how did they die?

Maybe I will learn more in the inquest reports, but of course the startling word, that I guess I must have at some level known would be there, is the word 'murder', seeing it in print for the first time and linked to my aunt, no soft soaping the words, no accident here, just plain murder.

MY UNCLE

I was interested to discover when my uncle died,

just to understand a little about his onward journey and have now located his death certificate. He outlived his wife and children by forty-four years, dying in the year 2000 at the advanced age of eighty-eight in the west country. He moved far away from the area of his notoriety, which is very understandable. I wonder how he managed his memories.

Did he immerse himself in another family to drown out the pain? He was, it seems, nearly ten years older than my aunt, he would have been forty-two when she died, by the standards of the 1950s quite old to start another family, but I am trying to uncover what happened next for him. My view of him is changing, I see him now as a very tragic man and I would like to know he found some way to heal his demons.

The death certificate shows that he died of cancer in a local hospital and his death was registered by a woman living a few streets away from him, who was resident at her address for a further seventeen years. I can find no trace of her after this, she must therefore have been considerably younger than him, there is also a husband at her address, so without the possibility of further information we must assume she was perhaps a carer/housekeeper of sorts, as that would fit the story. He is shown as a retired shop manager, so he kept to his career at the time of my aunt's death.

Extensive investigations by both me and my helpful researcher Elizabeth have not found any record of a marriage to my uncle other than that to my aunt. The family mythology had him remarrying, which I disclosed in part one, but this seems to be just that, mythology. He did not remarry or have any further children, so all my conjecture about him is wrong. He may have had relationships but felt unable to remarry, we need to remember he was a Catholic born in the first part of the 20th Century, so I think it unlikely he would have co-habited with anyone.

Each time I find out something new about my uncle, he shifts in my mind. I see him more clearly now, as a man broken by his loss, unable to start again. I have searched through the wills and probate grants on record for the period he died and the following year, in case a will could shed light on any wider family connections, but there is nothing on register, so it seems, sadly, he had nothing left to bequeath. His financial struggles were clearly with him for the rest of his life.

I looked at google maps to see his home, it was a very basic rather rundown property and as he left nothing in a will, we can only assume he must have been renting it.

I know my family did not keep in contact with him for long, which seems hard as they shared the loss. It may have helped him, yet it seems he was never good enough for my family and they laid blame at his door for what happened. I wish I had done this research sooner; I could have met him and made my own judgement and maybe represented for him my family taking back the judgement and offering him absolution. I will need to find my own way to make my peace with him.

I recalled, as I was writing this today, my first visit to the grave and seeing the words 'forever in dad's thoughts' written along the bottom of the headstone. I am sorry to say I did not give this much thought back then, but now I look at the picture I took of the gravestone and consider him choosing his words for the engraving and what it must have felt like for him as he stood by that graveside, on perhaps a spring like day, looking down at his family laid to rest beneath the soil.

I was so wrapped in my own perceived loss, the pain of my beloved family, I did not consider this man, this dad, perhaps I was influenced by my family's dismissal of him, blame of him, which I now perceive as a bit of projection, an inability to face their own mistakes. So now I do acknowledge him, this man who in fact never did remarry or start again. At least my family had me, a small investment in the next generation, a child to love again, what did he have? Maybe, I hope, some nephews and nieces, I feel this is something I will never know but let's hope so.

My grandfather dying from the shock of the tragedy needs to be viewed as hyperbole within the family mythology. I now find he outlived his daughter and grandchildren by five years, he died of pneumonia in 1959. Though he may well have had reduced immune function from the stresses of recent years, or he lost the will to fight to stay alive, as pneumonia was not the death sentence it had once been by this time, I think we can accept the events of 1954 may have hastened his death.

My grandfather was man who had flown biplanes over a war-torn France under fire in 1914, had been shot down once and survived, who had coped with the strain of recruiting agents to be dropped over France in another war, knowing he was sending them into extreme danger and potentially torture and death. He was a man who was cut off from part of his family in the Second World War, his parents, sister-in-law, nephew and nieces all living under German occupation, he had not known if they were dead or alive for six years, finally the loss of his daughter and grandchildren becomes the last blow in a difficult life.

His death would have been a terrible loss to an already shattered family. Now that my mother is finally opening-up about the past, she told me that she had known my father for three months before my grandfather died, though sadly she had not yet met him.

My mother regrets not having had the chance to meet my grandfather, as his reputation as a good man and a war hero cast a long shadow over the family. I felt my father struggled to live up to his reputation, as he followed his father into the French Air Force to do his military service, trying to make him proud. I have seen letters between father and son that showed this did not come easily to him, especially with the rest of his immediate family still in England and the problems in Algiers at the time leading to French soldiers returning in body bags.

I am glad to know that my father had already begun his relationship with my mother at the time of his father's death, as it must have given him some hope for the future at a time when he must have still been very raw with emotion and stuck in a marriage in which he was clearly unhappy.

I had not given much thought to my grandfather's role in the tragedy as we never met, and he was meant to quickly exit the picture with his sudden death. I need to review this now, how he lived on for a while with his grief and perhaps his own share of the guilt too. I regret that we never met and cling to the few stories that I have of him. One I remember is of him returning to France just after the second world war and attending a meeting at the Credit Lyonnais bank to assist with merging the British and French enterprises again. At this meeting he was introduced to a man who was a known collaborator during the war. The man went to shake his hand and my grandfather refused to shake it saying, 'There are many things in life that I have no control over, but one thing I can do is keep my hands clean'. I think this short story gives a sense of a proud man with a sense of honour. I see him standing straight backed with dignity. How his world must have been ripped apart by his daughter's actions.

Chapter six

THE HEADLINES

As I had failed in my newspaper quest, I looked for a researcher and found a very helpful woman in Canterbury in south-east England, who located five references in the digitised archives of British newspapers. Sadly, not every paper is there and the one I wanted most was not. When Elizabeth contacted me and said she had found the headlines, I was shaken, it meant the stories about the tragedy making it into the press were true, it meant I had to read the reports now that I had come this far. More facing of reality for me.

When I knew they were sitting there for me to read in my inbox, I was suddenly unsure. I remember saying 'oh my god, oh my god' several times out loud and feeling many mixed emotions, anticipation at finally seeing the truth, fear of what that might be and of course some residual guilt at breaking the promise I made to my father. I had waited to do this for years, to find some real answers, it was now very daunting. In the end I emailed them through to my partner to read first, so someone was prepared to support me through the revelations, and we would then discuss it together over the phone. I was not sure I wanted to be with it on my own, in fact, I knew as I faced it, I could not do it on my own.

The first headline is from *The People*, so this was the national publication my father had seen. I realised it could not have been *The Mirror* once I found out my aunt had died on a Saturday. It is not the top story, but the headline reads:

'Letter to her man – then death' proves to be the least salacious, but why is she sending her husband a letter? This was printed the day immediately after it happened, perhaps it was a blessing that it was a weekend, as there were less publications on a Sunday.

The one that made me freeze on the spot was the *Aberdeen Evening Express* 28th April 1954, printed after the inquest: 'Murdered three, then suicide. Inquest on mother and children'

Seeing the word murder again here in black and white in a newspaper, so very public, speaking of someone in my family was very disturbing.

The Birmingham Post 29th April 1954 said: 'Mother murdered her three children'

Liverpool Echo 28th April 1954: 'Killed her three children, then herself. Woman's last letter, a living death', so a killer now. Is that worse than a murderer? Now we know there is a letter, which should give some insight.

The Birmingham Gazette 26th April 1954: 'Three children in bed had been drowned'. So now I knew that all three children had been drowned, a real shock.

These are the articles we were able to find, one from as far away as Aberdeen, so it was a national news story and really brings home to me how awful it must have been to everyone who had known the family. The image of journalists outside the house was clearly a true one and you can imagine the gossip within their community. Judgement on the family she grew up in, what had made this woman from such a good home a murderer, capable of killing her own children, one of the truly worst crimes people can imagine. There may have been feelings like, what could her husband have done to drive her to this, as this had indeed been my feeling for many years.

I can almost sense the bewildered confusion of the family, as their world fell apart and turned into a nightmare. Judgements upon the family that were still clearly there decades later, as we saw when my father went back to the area the family had lived in and being confronted by it all yet again.

Chapter seven

THE INQUEST

THE NOTE

Reading the inquest report, we discover that there was a note/letter, sent to her husband, though only part of this was read out at the inquest which was held just four days after the bodies were found. Here is the extract:

'Don't come home as usual on Saturday, as by that time I shall have taken steps I have been contemplating for years. I have been enduring a living death for several years and cannot think of any alternative. I am sorry to take the children, but I have my reasons. '

We can only wonder if another letter was sent to her parents or brother, or if the part of the note not read out at the inquest could have been addressed to them. I wonder if it languishes in some police file somewhere or whether it was disposed of decades ago.

There is something significant about her

sending this note to her husband, rather than leaving it in the house. She clearly does not want him to walk in and find them all, she wants to save him from this, so there is some care there, some consideration, she also apologises for taking the children.

The language is interesting, saying 'taking', it sounds like she is running away with them to go to another country, rather than killing them. When he received the note, he called the police station near his family home and their response was to go to the house. So where was he to be sent this note? Well, it transpires that the gentleman's outfitters he managed was around seventy miles from his home, much nearer to his parents' house, so he stayed with his parents during the week and went home at the weekend, on a Saturday after work and stayed until Monday, so he had essentially one day a week with his family.

One of the report's states that he was in the shop in Watford where he worked when he received the news of the deaths. I imagine the scene in my mind's eye as he opens the note, disbelieving, calling the police and showing the note with shaking hands. Then he waits to hear what has happened, he waits, wondering what she has done, maybe just maybe she changed her mind, maybe they are all at home enjoying the usual bustle on a Saturday morning. I wonder if he immerses himself in his work, serving a customer or two, perhaps he has staff he can leave this to as he sits in the back of the shop. Did he tell his parents who are nearby? Did they rush over to be with him whilst he waited? Or maybe he held onto the fear and apprehension alone, waiting, waiting just in case it was all alright. I see him holding off telling anyone, holding on to scraps of hope, not wanting to vocalise the fear and make it real.

Then that moment he is told, I see him smartly dressed, after all he needs to be a good advertisement for the shop, standing up straight, an old soldier bracing himself for the news. He can see it is not good. I see him fighting to keep control of his emotions and not break down in front of the officer. I see him confused, not understanding, wrestling with the enormity of it, can it really have happened? Wondering how he will tell everyone, his parents, her parents.

I have often wondered, did he tell my grandparents or did the police head over to them on that Saturday afternoon, I will never know. Nothing in their life experience could prepare my grandparents for this, two world wars behind them, but nothing like this. I see my grandfather answer the door, ushering the police into the sitting room, taking the news first. I see this in my mind's eye, he hustles them out, she must not hear it from them, he looks for his wife to tell her, how will he tell her, how will he find the words for this?

I see her later that day in the church, I know the

73

church well, down on her knees begging for the soul of her daughter, for her lost grandchildren, never to really to rise from those knees, a constant supplication to God, begging her God. I marvel at her faith, but it was all she had left to cling to and her husband too, I think she clung to him. Bewildered, confused, and lost. I see them all like this, blinking in the light, unbelieving at first, then distraught. How can it be anything less? I have never faced this before, looked at it up close before and with the looking I find so much more understanding.

THE DISCOVERY

So, having sent the note to her husband to prevent him coming home, all my speculation about the discovery of the bodies has been wrong. It was in fact the police that broke into the property to find out if anything had happened there. So, it was not someone who knew them, which is a blessing, though even a hardened policeman would struggle with his emotions finding three dead children. It would haunt anyone and no doubt we should include these poor officers in our list of people affected by the tragedy.

One of the reports refers to the police breaking into the flat. This changes the impression from the address on the death certificate which gives a house number and not a flat. The building is currently a house but may indeed have been flats in the 1950s. It sounds from the description of the finding of the children that they all slept in one room, so perhaps it was a two bedroomed flat, quite a small space for an impending family of six.

MY UNCLE AWAY

So, my aunt was alone during the week with the three children and with another child due. If she was suffering from depression this may have been the thing that pushed her over the edge. The mention of his parents brought another thought to mind for me, there were of course others affected by these tragic deaths, the children had this other set of grandparents whose life would have been blighted with loss, perhaps not carrying the guilt that went through my family, but they carried a horrific loss.

How blinkered I was not to consider his wider family. He could have had siblings who were also uncle or aunt to those children and who shared in the loss. The ripples of grief move ever wider. My uncle's family may have had an additional dominant emotion, anger, anger towards my aunt for taking the children away and devastating their son/brother's life.

One question the coroner asked my uncle was 'did you ever give your wife cause for jealousy?', 'No' he replied, 'we were devoted'. It seems the coroner perhaps felt his absence may have had another cause than simply convenience and though it would be easy for me to blame him for these absences and blame them on another woman, I really do not feel this to be true. There was no hint of this in my family mythology and I am sure if there were any chance of an affair, they would have clung to it as they looked for excuses for what my aunt had done.

I have looked at a map to consider her sense of isolation. None of the family had cars in the 1950s, so all travel was by train. My uncle and his parents were two and half hours away by train, a journey that required at least two train changes. So, if he finished work at say 5pm on the Saturday he would have been home quite late and needed to leave very early on the Monday morning to be at work in time, so they had one day a week together as a family. My grandparents were as far away, around two and a half hours.

As there was no accommodation for guests, it would have been a five-hour round trip for a visit. My father was the same distance away too. So, all the support systems of two sets of grandparents, and her own brother were all concentrated a long way away in north London and into Middlesex. As I plotted it on the map, she really was out on a limb in her location. As she also went for the latter part of her education to a school in North London and worked in that area before marriage any long-term friendships would also have been a long way away.

Another observation is, that I had thought he was from Essex and that is why they were so far away from her family, but he was relatively local to where she grew up, so we can wonder how they ended up on the edges of Essex. If, for example, he had gone there for a job and it had not worked out, why did he not move his family back to their original area? The only conclusion I can come up with is money.

Maybe it would have been more expensive to live around that Watford area and the costs of moving were too great, but the cost turned out to be much higher. As I sat staring at the map, seeing so clearly that separation from all she knew, imagining her stuck there, day in day out, with limited visitors due to the distance, with three children under ten and one on the way, I felt angry again, but in a new way. Angry with my family and her husband. They all let her down. No wonder there was the secrecy and the guilt. No wonder. Perhaps they were as afraid of me judging them, as judging her.

THE CHILDREN

It is hard to read the inquest account of the children, as I have far too vivid an imagination. We saw on the death certificate that Keith had been drowned, and then from the headlines that all three children had been drowned. The boys were found neatly dressed in fresh pyjamas and were in their beds, which were side by side and their hair was still damp. Carol was likewise in fresh night clothes with damp hair, but she was in a cot, in the same room.

I had somehow imagined them being given a sedative and quietly smothered as they slept, awful, but more bearable than these drownings, she must have dressed them once they were already dead, as the hair is wet and the pyjamas dry.

I have wrestled with the idea of how you drown three children without them creating a fuss or trying to stop her. I just do not know; I cannot begin to understand how this unfolded that Friday evening as she prepared them for bed. We can wonder if they went obediently for their bedtime bath and it all happened too fast for them to truly understand the horror of what was happening, though too often I see Keith struggling as the oldest to save his little brother and sister, it really does not bear thinking about, though perhaps my imagination is too fertile, she may have simply taken them to the bathroom one by one, we will never know. That said, putting that awful struggle behind us, I can somehow see a tenderness in the way she lays them out on their beds. As I visualise the end scene, I imagine her kissing them as if she had just put them to bed and maybe that is how she was seeing it herself, as if she were just sending them into a deep, peaceful sleep, but the actual deaths can have been far from peaceful.

Keith was nine, Graham was six and Carol was three.

My aunt's body

We know already of course that my aunt gassed herself in the oven when coal gas was used. That image of a woman with her head in a gas oven, kneeling on the floor to reach in, seems to be one of the 1950s somehow, at least it is for me, though I have no idea where it comes from, an old black and white movie perhaps or an overheard conversation. I am sure I have seen it in a film, or maybe I have just imagined it this way for so long, it feels like I have seen it elsewhere.

Though it was not quite as neat as that, she was found lying on the kitchen floor, she was also found to have a deep cut on her left wrist believed to have been made by a safety razor. There was a lot of blood all over the kitchen floor. She was not leaving anything to chance, she was very determined to die, though having killed her children first, there was no way she could have changed her mind, she could not have stayed, it clearly had to be the end. So, she tried with the razor at first and failed so then resorted to the oven.

THE TIME-LAG

One of the very difficult pieces of evidence for me is the time lag between the children's deaths and her own. The children had been dead between twelve to eighteen hours when they were found, so this ties in with a bedtime late on the Friday evening. She had been dead just two to three hours when the police arrived. She must have been up all through the night and killed herself on the Saturday morning.

That night must have been living hell for a tormented mind having done such a terrible act. I struggle to go anywhere near those thoughts in my mind. Was it like that, or was she sitting by their beds, perhaps stroking their hair, and watching over them, did she want this peaceful last time with them, dreading the final act of leaving them? I veer between the two images, the tormented screaming, crying distress and the peaceful mother watching over her children, almost unaware of what she had done, spending those last precious moments with them until she was ready to go.

NO FINANCIAL WORRIES

It is interesting that my uncle states to the coroner that they have no financial worries. We do not have the full context of the discussion, so maybe the coroner asked directly about their finances, maybe my uncle said all was well to save face. There had no doubt been financial problems which must have affected his pride. An inability to take care of your family was particularly damning in those times when men worked, and women mostly stayed at home.

The fact that they had problems is not hearsay, I have seen the evidence in the letters to my father in which my aunt is asking for money for very basic needs. It may have been that this job that involved him being away during the week had been the turning point for them as a family financially and therefore he must have hoped things would now get better, perhaps he had been unemployed for a while before this.

It must have been galling for him to accept money from his wife's younger brother who would have been nearly twenty years his junior and would no doubt have created some tensions in the family home. I have wondered if they argued about it, a husband asking his wife not to tell her brother they needed money and her pleading that they had not enough money to feed and clothe the children, that he would have to forego his pride and let her ask, or did she do it secretly behind his back, we will never know, but these financial worries must have added to the family tensions.

We can also note that at this time rationing was still in force and if you did not have the money to buy on the black market, you would be managing a very limited range of foods. Their finances would not have been under such strain if they did not have so many children and yet another due. So, we assume loyal to her Catholic faith, she did not practice contraception, to not limit the chances of a life, however this led her to do something so much worse in the eyes of her god and end up judged by anyone hearing her story.

Moody

Some small amount of light is shed on my aunt's mental health at the inquest when her husband describes her as 'moody' and 'had had a bad pregnancy with the girl'.

I have to jump in here and say these are his words, he does not use his daughter's name, he does not say she had a bad pregnancy with Carol.

We can consider whether he is distancing himself from his grief or whether he was not very connected to his children. The couple of photos that still exist of him with the children show a smiling loving man, but I suppose anyone can smile for a camera.

We clearly have post-natal depression here and perhaps, as she is pregnant, some pre-natal depression too. In different times a health visitor or midwife might have flagged up some concerns. There is no mention in the reports of the inquest that she was pregnant. This may have been to protect the feelings of her husband, or out of some sort of nod towards some unspoken rule of decency at the time. Maybe there had not been a post-mortem as the cause of death was obvious, having been found with her head in the oven and the room filled with gas, in which case the court would not have known about the pregnancy.

One of the cousins in France was adamant that my aunt was pregnant at the time of her death according to my mother. We cannot know whether this had been a private confidence between the two cousins or whether it was more widely known within the family, but this must surely have been the tipping point. My mother said that my father never mentioned that she had been pregnant, I hope he never knew on one level though it might have brought more understanding.

There is no record of a report being made by her own doctor, which I find staggering. Though their funds were limited, it was during the early days of the National Health Service, so there should have been some medical support for her. It seems astounding that someone could do such an act and there be no reference to their previous medical history and current situation.

The only medical evidence is from the doctor that certified the deaths at the scene. Her husband is asked at the inquest if she had shown any sign that she was enduring a living death, he said they were devoted and that she had never threatened to take her own life. If that were the case, why was her husband's first thought when he got the note in the post that she had done something like this and send the police to the house, rather than thinking she may have left him and that is what she meant by taking the children.

This living death she refers to, could be due only to the pre/post-natal depression or it could be the terrible isolation she felt. The lack of mental stimulation and fulfilment for someone who was reputed to be extremely bright may also play a part in the situation. It is interesting that she says, 'a living death' and not 'a living hell' from such wording there is no implied judgement of him, no indication that he has been difficult to live with in these words, even the insinuations of Cousin Jackie do not show in these words. It really reads like someone with a deep clinical depression.

REFERENCE TO EASTER

In his evidence to the coroner my uncle states after saying they are devoted, 'We spent the happiest Easter in all the years of our married life'. My first thought when I read this was that he was saving face again, he must have felt judged by everyone in the court for his wife to do such a thing, but then I thought about it some more. I checked when Easter was in that year, and it was the weekend immediately before the deaths. He probably would have had an extra day with the family for Easter Monday, the children were dead by the Friday.

If my aunt had reached the decision that she was planning her escape, distorted, and disturbed as that escape route was, it may well be that she felt good that weekend knowing it was all to end soon, she could enjoy her last weekend with her husband and children. It is not unusual for someone when their partner is leaving them to report afterwards that things were so good just before. This is of course a very extreme case of this, but if we accept his word, then it is the only explanation that fits the situation.

If this was indeed the case, it makes his experience even more tragic. He has this great weekend with the family, feels the tide is finally turning and his wife's depression receding, he begins to feel life for him is more worth living and then he is hit with this unimaginable loss. When one re-reads the note, imagining him in his shop receiving it and sending the police to check on the house, her previous depression must have manifested as bad enough for him to fear the worst.

My uncle now cuts for me an even more tragic figure, with every new piece of information I gain, as I see him in my mind again and again waiting in his shop for news of his family. The culpable villain that I had conjured in my head over the years to justify her behaviour to myself has all but disappeared. I see a man of limited means and experience grappling with a situation he did not understand, having been made to feel for years not good enough for her and now, look what she does to him. The bewilderment he must have felt after that lovely easter weekend, followed by the rage and the pain.

THE VERDICT

The jury found that a thirty-three-year-old woman murdered her three children and then took her own life whilst the balance of her mind was disturbed. So that is the end of the story for my aunt and her three children and the beginning of the trauma for everyone involved, the inquest behind them, the verdict in black and white. Now they had to learn to live with what my aunt had done and their perceived roles in the tragedy.

Chapter eight

MORE NEW FACTS

MY FATHER'S FIRST MARRIAGE

Another subject not discussed in the family, was my father's first marriage. I can remember when I found out my father had been married before. I was looking in a tin trunk in which he had lots of papers stored and I found letters addressed to a different Mrs Thomelin to my mother. Somewhat surprised I went to my father and asked who this might be. I was about fourteen when I discovered he had an ex-wife.

I raised the question in part one about when I was told about my aunt, as I have no clear memory of it. I do have a glimmer of memory that there were also letters addressed to my aunt from my father and hers to him stored in this trunk, a memory that shimmers on the edge of my awareness, though I am no longer sure I trust all my memories as I seem to have filled in many gaps over the years, as we do when we are trying to make sense of things. But perhaps it was at this point too when I found out about what had happened to my aunt, but I have clearly a big block in my memory about this.

I moved into an angry mode in my teens about this first wife, especially when I then discovered she even featured in some of our family photograph albums. This did not sit comfortably with me, this view of my father having another life before ours and it seemed to cloud other revelations at the time.

A possessiveness of my father was strong in me, and I did not want to be sharing him with an ex-wife. To have these two revelations about my family during my adolescence led to me having to readjust my world view and I had really stumbled into the revelations at a time when perhaps I was not quite old enough to process them, or perhaps not given enough information to process them properly.

My mother has finally talked to me about this previous marriage, and I am getting closer to the facts of it. I do not know where I got this impression, but I had believed he was married at the time of my aunt's death and it was that which created tensions between them, leading to the opening for my mother. But it now appears this is not true and that they married just afterwards, apparently his then girlfriend threatened my father that if he did not marry her, she would commit suicide, not a very fair card to play under the circumstances and this must have been hard for him to handle.

His sister's death would have been very raw, it seems they married a year after his sister's death. The only thing my father ever said to me about the marriage, and this was much later in life, was that he had known her for a long time from the church community, she had gone to the girl's school that was a sister to his own school and that he knew as he stood beside her to marry her that it was wrong. This difference in timing is interesting, it seems I need to adjust again the story that I told myself. I wondered whether I needed a reason for my father to be unfaithful to his wife with my mother.

The tragedy felt a good reason for the marriage to break down as he plunged into despair and needed a new start, five years of a loveless marriage a less agreeable one to an idealistic teenager who worshipped her father. It interests me that we can build up firm pictures, ideas and memories in our minds that we repeat to ourselves again and again and they become our truths. I would have said I was certain he was married at the time of the tragedy.

Most of the time these distortions of the past do not really matter, but as I tell this story of my family and all its ramifications, you can see there are essential truths in there but in some places, they are quite distorted and that can affect our behaviours and responses to a whole range of situations. I wonder how many families have their myths that filter through the generations, that alter the future outcomes of each family member without them even realising it. I hope through reading my family story it can help people to shine a light on their family, find the truths and dispel the myths.

WHY DID MY AUNT TAKE THE CHILDREN WITH HER?

Even now, suicide is a taboo in our society, though we are working hard to open discussion about it to help family survivors and reduce the large numbers of suicides we experience particularly in the UK. I think anyone reading my aunt's story might understand why she would in a dark moment consider taking her own life, we have at least got that far in our understanding of mental health. But taking the children to their death with her sends a shudder through the mind of the most tolerant soul.

I have over the years felt able to say I had an aunt who committed suicide, but I only tell those I have known a long time and feel close to that she killed her children too; it is rather a conversation stopper.

It had been convenient for me over the years to blame her killing the children on her husband, to assume that if she had left the children behind, she was leaving them in the hands of a violent man or an abuser, thus she was keeping them safe. This is now clearly, with evidence, untrue. She would not have apologised in the note for taking them if he was in any way dangerous and indeed, she might have alluded to that in the note to exonerate her own behaviour, but the only explanation we get is that she has her reasons.

I have researched why women kill their children, it often seems to be when they are suffering post-natal depression, or the result of psychosis from drug abuse or mental illness like schizophrenia. The fact that she states that she has her reasons means, though they may be distorted, she had some idea why she was doing it rather than just reacting on the spur of the moment.

The tenderness in the way she lays the children on the beds in their clean pyjamas is not a violent or angry killing as you might see with for example drug abuse, though drowning is not the gentlest way to kill them. Maybe she had no access or even money to pay for sedative drugs that might have been a more peaceful way to have done it.

There are a few scenarios I can imagine here, the first being that she simply did not want to be parted from her children and in some distorted way she felt they would be going together into some after life. She was it seems a committed Catholic but how this sits with the church's view on suicide as a mortal sin that will send you to hell alongside the sins of killing, I cannot quite reconcile, but she was not in a rational state and maybe she did feel she was 'taking' them to a better life. This idea does sit well with the language she uses in the note.

Another thought is that she was possessive of them, did not want to leave them in someone else's care, they were her children, and she did not want to be replaced by another mother if her husband were to remarry, or perhaps she saw her husband as incapable of caring for them and imagined them ending up in social care.

My aunt had already asked her mother to help, and she had said no, so perhaps she could not see the children being cared for by their grandparents. There is of course the stigma of growing up the child of a parent who commits suicide and all the abandonment issues that go with it, maybe she felt she was protecting them from this.

We can come up with many different interpretations about why she did it, I am at last old enough and experienced enough from the work I do as a therapist now to understand the despair of a broken mind, the illogical processing of such a mind and I can at last accept that she was responsible for this act and not look for scapegoats and to no longer judge her for that act. She was undoubtedly let down by the health system, she must have been very mentally unwell and was unsupported, there is no mention of medication or treatment of her pre/post-natal depression.

Her husband and family as I have already said

let her down too, they did not understand how critical the situation was and we have to judge them as we do her from the position of the time this happened, when there was much less understanding of mental health issues.

This tragedy happened not long after the war so there were many men who must have had PTSD from what they had experienced, especially those that had liberated the concentration camps. If there was no support for them, what chance is there for an isolated woman battling with her depression.

It has been very important for me to make peace with my aunt, to find the real story and work through my understanding of what happened. I can only wish that my father and grandmother could have had suitable mental health support of their own, to help them deal with this family tragedy and things may have been different for me. If they had felt able to tell me the whole story, I would not have created this myth that I might be like her and hurt myself when I was a teenager.

If I had known about the depression she had suffered related to her pregnancies, it would have stopped me making any link to my own experience. In the end my father and grandmother steeped themselves in the church, which no doubt helped them in its own way but reinforced ideas of sins and punishments that may have contributed to their health issues and certainly took much of the joy out of life for them.

MY NIGHTMARES

You may remember in part one, my description of a symptom linked to Parkinson's Disease, which causes confusion on waking, the transition from dream to wakefulness is undefined and it takes some time to realise what is really happening.

I often feel it must be like the confusion of dementia. Whilst writing this section of the book, where I have been reading the newspaper reports I have had a repetitive waking dream.

Usually, I get these about once a fortnight, but this has been every night for a week now. Each night I have woken between one and three in the morning with the feeling there is something vital I must do which is a matter of life and death. I do not know what it is that I am supposed to be doing but I know it is very important, it leads to me jumping out of bed and pacing around trying to remember what it is that is so important, then gradually, slowly the questioning begins and I realise after about fifteen minutes that I have been in one of my waking dreams and I climb back into bed and try to calm my racing heart.

As it is our subconscious that generates the dream state, we can see my subconscious at work here, the timing of these dream states indicates how the responsibility for this family situation has been handed on to me. It is my turn to feel I should have rescued them, the life and death action I cannot quite remember, it is now my role, only I am a few decades too late. Perhaps this was what pursued my father in his nightmares too, the need to act and then the realisation it is too late.

So, now I seem to be acting out the family trauma in my dreams instead of it being hidden away, maybe this is part of the process to finally let it go. I do not want to take on this responsibility, it is not mine to take, I was not there to let her down and maybe I would have too and maybe I would not, but it is not my story anymore, I am handing it back.

Now I need to continue my therapeutic journey, I already feel huge liberation through the writing and the processing that the truth has brought, though I am having to adjust my perspectives a lot. These waking dreams do show some sort of shift and my anger at this legacy fuels me further into the need for change. I want to manage my own health symptoms and, in some way heal this terrible rip/tear in my family. Even though I am the last of the line it still feels incumbent on me to affect some closure for all of us.

Part Two

The Effects of Generational Trauma
and the Therapeutic Approach to it

Chapter nine

THE IMPACT OF TRAUMA

We have looked at the very personal story of my family trauma to illustrate how a trauma can affect family members from different generations. There is a lot of interest now in generational trauma, sometimes referred to as transgenerational or intergenerational trauma. It is the passing of a traumatic experience down through the generations when the individual suffering has not had the appropriate support for their experience or been able to process it and is therefore unable to contain the impact of it. We will be considering whether this kind of inherited trauma is possible and if that trauma is purely psychological or could have some impact on the physical health of family members.

Much of the information and research in this area surrounds holocaust survivors and is usually the first point of reference for any investigation. It seems to be now generally accepted that there can be a psychological impact which can transfer beyond the first generation. As research has shown, grandchildren of holocaust survivors are 300% more likely to access psychiatric services than the normal level within the population.

However, the most powerful understanding for me, comes through real human stories rather than just statistics. Emily Wanderer Cohen has done some wonderful work highlighting the issues through storytelling. She is a child of a holocaust survivor, she stated that her mother managed to terrify her even as an adult with her anger and rages, her mother's descriptions of the terrible world we live in left Cohen always imagining the worst that could happen. Her mother felt a need to not draw attention to herself, not take the blame for anything and be perfect in the concentration camp. This led to a perfectionism in her that Cohen struggled to live up to and then not to pass on to her own children.

The most impactful words that leaped off the page at me when reading the book, were that she forgave her mother. It feels very important to acknowledge that this is not a story of blame. All we are trying to do is understand the impact of these traumas and to heal from them, as Cohen is trying to do with her work and I with mine. As we individuals, who are affected by such trauma tell our stories and raise more awareness, then hopefully, we can begin to stop the next generations travelling the same path as us and perhaps also generate more support for those suffering with PTSD, so it is less likely to impact on the wider family.

The potential areas of risk for transgenerational trauma can be seen to be wide ranging. There is a growing awareness of the impact of colonialism, the atrocities, and depravations it brought within communities and the resulting social implications related to these experiences. We can consider the soldiers fighting in wars around the globe, seeing and doing things no-one should have to see and do, coming home and trying to settle into normal family life. I have worked with such people, and they need real support not to pass their trauma down the line.

I live in the UK close to the channel and refugees are arriving on our shores daily, facing the risk of death to get here and then the lack of social inclusion on arrival, how can these survivors of conflict, fleeing for their lives, not risk passing their trauma on to the families they will have here?

These examples may seem obvious, but what about the individual smaller constituency, the people who have had a family member raped or murdered? These stories are sadly too common in our society, the scale whether small like this or huge like the survivors of the holocaust, all face the risk of generational trauma, the structures of support and plans for treatment are limited and the understanding of the scale of this work is only just beginning.

Could there be a difference between the impacts on a large scale, such as communities that have experienced oppression compared to those individual cases of tragedy impacting on family? I am not sure whether it is just a case of scale, but we are a long way from knowing the answer to this.

We do not need to limit ourselves to the impact on the victims of trauma. Those that could be descended from what we could call perpetrators can be affected too. Nora Krug explores this in her book *Belonging*. In this she examines what it means to be of German descent and how it affected her sense of belonging. She did not want to feel connected to a culture capable of the atrocities of the concentration camps, despite being born long after the end of the second world war.

Krug found herself when living in America steering away from German ex-pat communities, she reflects on the responsibility we need to take for our country's past and acknowledges that she must confront the past of her own family, coming to terms with having an uncle who was in the SS, to accept, in a sense, her German identity and the associated collective guilt that comes with it. The actions of our ancestors will impact upon us in some way, the wisdom comes in examining it and finding a way to make peace with it in a way that works for us as an individual and not transmit a faulty relationship with the past into the next generation.

The family we are born into teach us the most important learnings we have, we will learn to walk by watching and copying those around us, we listen and try to say words, picking up the language, tone and accent of the adults around us, we are a learning sponge picking up all that we can consciously and subconsciously about the world we have been born into by our main role models, our family. Until the age of seven we do not question the reality as presented to us by our family, our brain waves are in the alpha state, the learning state and so we learn.

I see in my clients every day the faulty learnings people acquire, such as their relationship with alcohol or food, or learned fears such as heights, spiders, and the like. I rarely see an anxious client who has not had at least one anxious parent, so there should be no surprise then, that we pick up other learnings, the learnings related to trauma, undercurrents of fear, insecurity, shame, guilt and blame, those beliefs that pervade the lives of those that have suffered trauma.

Dr Merzenich in his book *Soft Wired* looks at this when considering neuroplasticity and the learning process. He notes we are born without a clear identity, but we gradually upload new learnings and skills, each of which has a reference point when it is essentially filed, giving us our associations, and leading us to make predictions as to outcomes in various situations. If there is emotion attached to when we learned a piece of information, it will be there when we retrieve it.

The references we create essentially become personal to us, creating our own referential index, we will be taking the information around us, interpreting it and making it ours, but based on those inputs around us, for example we might smell freshly baking bread and it makes us feel secure because it reminds us of our grandmother's kitchen. This brings us to an idea that has recently been labelled the transgenerational atmosphere which gives us a context in which to place this learning.

Through our considerations already we can see that this learning is not just restricted to a family, it can stretch out into the culture we are born into. We must consider that if we do not have the full information to make our own judgements, we will fill in the gaps and create learnings which are perhaps not beneficial to us, rather like the fears I had as a teenager that could have been erased if I had known the full story about my aunt's situation which was so very different to my own.

Chapter ten

THE TRANSGENERATIONAL ATMOSPHERE

The idea of a transgenerational atmosphere has been developed by Tihamér Bahó and Katalin Zana. This resonates with me; I can see it as a miasma lurking beneath the surface of a family to infect and pollute it. This atmosphere is generated by the member/members of the family who have experienced the trauma first-hand, they unconsciously communicate the impact of the trauma within the family, this then becomes an intrinsic part of the learning within that family.

The original cause of the trauma is often hidden, a difficult secret, so there is no possibility for this trauma to be processed and healed. The family remain stuck in the past whilst trying to negotiate the present. Those that have not directly experienced the trauma find themselves fighting with shadows, held by the gossamer threads of a past they have no way of understanding, as the information is withheld from them.

Again and again, I read about traumas so great that the individual cannot hold it alone, they are passing on to their family their own unfiltered, unchallenged perspective of that trauma, their interpretations of that experience which may indeed be faulty. Gerard Fromm shares this view in his introduction to *Lost in Transmission*. Peter Loenburg, when talking of trauma he notes the origin of the word trauma, from the Greek for wound or injury.

When I read this, it had such resonance for family trauma, this gaping open wound, which is being ignored within the family so there can be no healing, it festers, like a damaged limb belonging to the family unit which holds it back, prevents it from developing as it should. I could visualise this wound in my family and see by not attending to it, it had become even more damaging than it was already inevitably going to be.

I note from my work with families that have experienced trauma and indeed my own experience, that those for whom the impact was greatest are so absorbed in their own suffering they cannot compute that it is affecting the wider family and the next generation or generations, it is in fact a rather selfish position, it is all about them and they cannot see further than that.

This position of self-absorption is part of the flight/flight response as when we are in this response, we disassociate to protect ourselves, we have to be the priority to maintain our survival. After a large trauma a person can remain in this dissociated state for some time or drift in and out of it. Again, no blame is being attached to this, but with the right support the individual can be helped to see beyond their own suffering.

Gabriele Schwab in her book *Haunting Legacies*, refers to the impact of trauma on the family as like a haunting that transmits across the generations. She had her own awakening to this concept, as she had a brother who had died before she was born, and she brought him into her fantasy world. Schwab carried the imprint of her brother's death though it was not something to discuss within the family and perhaps there could be in there some survivor's guilt, along with the burden of replacing a child that has gone before. She was aware that her brother had existed but was not given enough information to be able to process the loss.

I can relate to this concept of a haunting, I have felt haunted by the photograph that I started my story with, haunted by all it represented, it has always been there in the background, nothing solid, nothing I could seize upon but always there, a presence that seeped into our lives. This concept of replacement children, to which Schwab devotes a whole chapter, stimulated by this experience of her own quite honestly shook me.

I had felt the burden of the hopes of my father and grandmother of my dead cousins, the burden of being the survivor who had to do well, excel to make up for the loss, the weight of the next generation on my shoulders alone. It was a revelation to read of someone else who had a similar journey, an obvious connection to the outsider but not so obvious when you are busy living the experience.

When I first began to discuss the work that I was doing with my mother about our family trauma, she could not see that I would be affected by something that happened before I was born. She had watched my father suffer and understood his suffering, challenging though that had been at times, it was only through sensitive discussion she began to comprehend that it could have had an impact on me and indeed had affected her more than she would have previously acknowledged.

This event had happened before my mother met my father, yet it had affected the decades of life she shared with him. I am very proud of the depth of understanding she has worked through. When we find ourselves watching programmes on the television together, she will point out risk points within a family story that could lead to trauma, she is 88 and still learning and developing, there is hope for everyone, we can always access change given the right encouragement and understanding.

Chapter eleven

GENERATIONAL TRAUMA RISK FACTORS

When researching what is most likely to make a trauma pass across the generations, I come back to the work of Tihamér Bahó and Katalin Zana. They express the concept that trauma is most likely to pass beyond the current generation if the social environment around the trauma is not sympathetic or empathic. The overwhelming social revulsion to those that kill children and even worse the taboo surrounding killing your own children, makes the situation for my family ripe for handing that trauma down the generations. Indeed, they explain that silence rather than sharing an experience, not having the ability to share with others who have had similar experiences heightens the trauma for the individual and the risk of transmitting this even subconsciously grows. Schwab reflects on the silencing of trauma in her work and says that you cannot ever completely silence a trauma, it will always find its way out even if unconsciously.

The absence of safe expression of an experience, Baho and Zana argue affects the mourning process leading to a fragmenting of the experience, a suppression which prevents a healthy integration of what has happened, enhancing the impact and long-term effects of the trauma. I can see this suppression clearly in my family, the silence around it, yet with that photograph ever present, it was always there as a reminder of what was missing. We were not allowed to address it, to find a way to process and heal it, so it sat as an ever-present open wound within the family, weaving its way into the family narrative around things that have to remain hidden unspoken, cloaked in shame.

There was of course little public sympathy for the family of a child killer. It may have been easier for my uncle who is seen perhaps as the main victim of the story, though he may have experienced judgement and suspicion for his role in what happened. No-one comes out of this story who is close to it, into a safe space to heal.

There are so many environments which have historically not felt safe and induced trauma which could have been transferred. We can consider, for example, the young women in Ireland who became pregnant out of wedlock and had their children adopted via church organisations as highlighted in the film *Philomena*. The women were made to feel ashamed of their pregnancy and had guilt for giving away their children, they did not have a safe space to heal, in many it became a guilty secret, this is fertile ground for transgenerational trauma. How many of them have gifted guilt and shame onto their children, or perhaps clung too tightly to those children, as they had already lost a child. The impact of their experience if not dealt with cannot but help to impact their future family. I am hoping through the work that I am doing here, that people will see how their own trauma or past family trauma may have affected them and begin to find their way towards resolution.

The impact of trauma on a psychological level appears to be generally accepted, but new evidence shows that it can also be physical, that this too can be passed on through the generations. If we are going to understand the impact of trauma on my family, and the wider implications of trauma in so many families, we can perhaps start by looking at the mind - body connection and then into the wider context of how a traumatic experience can be shared within a family.

Chapter twelve

MIND - BODY CONNECTION

I went to a conference on Post Traumatic Stress Disorder some years ago and one of the delegates stood up and asked the question 'when did the medical profession decide to separate the mind from the body?', with the implication that we needed to put them together again.

Certainly, it is now accepted that PTSD can have a long-term impact on neuroplasticity, the nervous system and the immune system. It is important to acknowledge this point to be able to help people affectively and indeed to help ourselves.

We just have to examine the idea of the placebo, which most people would accept now, to see how what we believe can affect our body responses, for example in one trial people taking placebo antidepressants had an equal improvement to people taking a pharmaceutical intervention, in another a placebo for migraine was labelled the same as the real medication and proved as effective as the real medication. There are even sham operations that have shown the impact of belief on health, such as brain cell implants for people with Parkinson's Disease, which showed an improvement in the sham group, equal to that of those who had active treatment.

Conversely people can be affected by its opposite, the nocebo, where a negative suggestion can create bad physical responses, like someone given a medical diagnosis by mistake, their symptoms worsen, when there is no physical reason for that to happen.

The Technical University of Munich has done a study of all the research into the nocebo and raise concerns that this needs to be considered as a considerable risk factor, for example patients who are warned a particular test may increase their pain, often experience more pain than those who are given no such instruction. They reported an extreme case of someone attempting suicide, taking an overdose of tablets that were in fact placebos and becoming very ill and only recovering when he was told that the tablets were not pharmaceutical. His simple belief that the pills had the potential to harm him, made him dangerously ill.

In hypnotherapy we use tests called suggestibility tests, these are designed to assess the level of suggestibility of an individual. The tests usually involve a level of visualisation of an idea that then causes a physical response, for example:

We will get someone to stand with their eyes closed and their arms stretched out horizontally in front of them and to visualise that in one hand a large book has been placed, around the wrist of the other hand a light balloon has been tied, with skilful use of language and the addition of further imaginary books and balloons, the subject will find one hand falling and the other rising creating a wide gap between the height of the hands developing. When you get the subject to open their eyes they are always surprised at the change in the position of their arms, seeing how what they believed impacted upon them.

The most widely used suggestibility test is the lemon test, where you get someone to visualise the colour, texture, and shape of a lemon, then cut the lemon in half, raise it to their mouth and let the lemon juice run over the tongue. This in many people will stimulate a mouth-watering response due to the imagined sharpness of the lemon juice and often accompanying swallowing.

Let us substitute for suggestibility, the word belief, assessing our power to believe something enough for us to respond physically to that belief in the mind. If such simple visualisations can create a response in the action of the body, I believe that feelings like guilt and shame can impact on our physical health.

Some people might see their illness as a punishment or perhaps sometimes we can see it as the manifestation of distress and a call for help. If this is the case, then why not consider that this too can become a learned response.

One of the most obvious ways the mind affects the body is through the stress response which triggers all sorts of internal changes to function at the point of a perceived threat, but the mind decides on the level of threat and will trigger the response accordingly. In such a case, the blood flow is diverted away from the digestive system into the arms and legs to run or fight, the heart rate increases to support blood flow, the breathing increases to oxygenate the blood to be nourished for action, blood flow moves from the thinking forebrain to the survival hind brain so we can act more quickly, cortisol is released to prevent allergic reaction. To assist the ability to run the body can have diarrhoea, literally getting rid of excess baggage, this can also apply to the bladder, cholesterol is pumped into the bloodstream to provide a boost of energy for flight, and much, much, more, as the brain interprets danger and swings into action.

Our brain has been partially programmed by thought, as to what is and what is not a danger. This is an individual programming, which is why one person can have an anxiety attack whilst walking into a supermarket, being in a high place or seeing a spider, it is all part of the programming that the mind has created, but it generates a real physical response, that feels outside our conscious control.

In very simple terms we can consider the common cold. If we imagine a room full of people and one person has a head cold, not everyone in that room will get the cold, some will. What is different between those that do and that do not? Some will already have some immunity to the virus, some will fight it off with their immune system, but those who are highly stressed may find their immune system will not work effectively as the energy of the body systems are busy preparing to run and fight and diverted away from the immune function, leaving the body undefended.

We can take this up a notch towards getting something more serious like cancer. There are of course many factors that can influence the risk of cancer, but if you are very stressed and not managing that stress, you are increasing the risk of getting cancer as your immune system may be caught off guard.

Gabor Maté addresses the impact of stress upon the body in his book, *When the Body Says No*. He believes that the potentiality to be affected by stress in a way that brings more serious illness, is laid down early in life, the response to stress in our early lives setting up this pattern of over stimulation to that response. We learn about the world around us from the family we grow up in as we have already considered, they give us our template for the world, or our 'map of reality' to use NLP language.

If the information we are given in our family unit is influenced by trauma in the family, we will learn that the world is a scary place, imprinting onto our stress response that it needs to be hyper vigilant. Therefore, the trauma of someone else, is having a physical impact on our bodies, as we are responding to their experience. If then, you associate even subconsciously that illness is a part of that learned response to trauma, then you have a recipe for illness to become your response if you experience anything challenging in your life that you interpret as extremely stressful or traumatic. Maté seems to share my belief, citing that families generate a template for illness that can be shared through generations.

There is now an acceptance in the medical profession that some symptoms cannot be traced to a specific disease or accident and remain undiagnosed, as we now have a classification of medically undiagnosed symptoms (MUS) or sometimes referred to as medically undiagnosed physical symptoms (MUPS). This can lead people to feel their symptoms are not taken seriously or they are not believed. There is however a growing understanding that the mind - body relationship is more complex than we have hitherto understood and much more research needs to be done to support this work.

A paper published in 2017 evidenced that fifty

per cent of people suffering from PTSD, also suffered chronic pain. It seems to me an outward sign of the inner pain and suffering and only through treating the psychological pain can we hope to relieve the symptoms, though this does not mean we doubt the reality of the symptoms. Other research has evidenced that MUS is frequently experienced in those that have suffered trauma, across a range of areas, often linked to stress such as IBS and chronic pain. I say again that if we learn from a family member that a physical symptom is an outward expression of inner trauma, it seems possible that child could go on to have a history of illness when meeting life challenges.

The platform upon which much of the concept of the ability to alter the mind-body position stands upon is the work of Kandel from Columbia University Department of Psychiatry, this is particularly relevant I believe for trauma. Norman Doidge in his work *The Brain that Changes Itself* quotes extensively on this research as a basis for his work, he demonstrated synaptic connections could increase and neurones change their anatomical shape and through his work with snails, showing how they could learn fear and become hyper vigilant in the same way a human can display when having panic attacks and high anxiety.

If structures can be altered in this way, then can this be altered in the alternative direction? Can we begin to heal and change our body chemistry?

I want to make it clear here, that accepting that the mind and the body work together, whether to improve or damage function, there is no blame or fault attached to this as that connection is an unconscious one, that we have no direct control over, even less so if we consider in many cases, we have been gifted a faulty system by our early learning. Our antecedents did not understand that they were gifting us the wrong information. We need to find the route to healing the problem and hopefully stop sending the faulty information down the generations. Only through working with the subconscious/unconscious can we have the potential to affect some change for both the mind and the body.

If we accept that the mind can impact on the body and that there is strong evidence for trauma to be a contributary factor, we can look further into the transgenerational nature of trauma with both psychological and potentially physical impact.

Chapter thirteen

EPIGENETICS

We cannot consider the mind-body connection without examining the idea of Epigenetics which signposts the ability to make alterations through the mind body relationship and indeed provides us with some hope for the future, enabling us to understand the mechanism of that change.

I first encountered this subject when I was studying to be a hypnotherapist, my tutor introduced us to the work of Dawson Church. I remember reading case studies such as the story of a man who developed psoriasis. It was a serious case and was not responding well to treatment. The doctor who was convinced of the mind-body relationship asked questions about when the problem began. The doctor ascertained that the problem had started when the patient's girlfriend had told him she was pregnant. He had not made the connection to his reaction to the news, the doctor enabled him to understand why it had started. He was perhaps not feeling ready to become a father. The doctor then gave him some words to focus upon, he treated it by understanding the cause and then telling the psoriasis through mantra like repetition to go away. I was fascinated and wondered if it could really be that simple and how it would go on to influence the work that I would do.

I went on to discover the work of Bruce Lipton, the cellular biologist who gave tangible explanations for how this worked. I attended workshops he held in London twice and his research explained so much that we have instinctively known for a long time but not had the science to evidence it, which is simply the proof of the mind body connection. He explained that when the Human Genome project discovered that there were 25,000 genes in the human body, this was far lower than had been expected and could not account for the complexity of a human being, yet through epigenetic control this could be explained.

Lipton had been conducting experiments to ascertain what was causing behaviour within a cell, he discovered that perception was controlling the behaviour. DNA (genes) had been thought to be the most important aspect of each cell ever since Watson and Crick published their work on DNA in 1953.

Lipton explains that we now know it to be the blueprint for making protein in the cell, environmental factors then drive the protein of every cell, which has perception switches on it, the

DNA itself does not have an on/off switch. As a result of these perception switches on the proteins, a variety of behaviours can be the result, as one gene can provide 2000 different behaviours, so the blueprint can be altered.

What does this all mean? What this means is that if you have a gene for a particular health issue, it does not guarantee it will become active, it needs a trigger via the perception switches, for example you can have the lung cancer gene but not get lung cancer as you did not trigger it by smoking, now that is a clear and practical example, but also the belief that you will get the disease as a family member has had it, could be just as damaging for you. He argues that the triggers can be organic or from the impact of the mind, of belief.

At one of his London workshops, he argued that only one per cent of disease is caused by genetics, he argued that it is our belief that determines our biology. In our minds those beliefs are often negative, the mind drifts towards a negative bias, so we are more likely to create more negative outcomes for ourselves.

Nurture turns out to have as important, if not even a more important role than nature, how we perceive the world will affect our biology. Trauma, toxins and thought all have their role to play in the outcome.

Since I discovered these ideas, I wondered if Descartes famous quote 'I think therefore I am' should be more like 'How I think dictates how I am'. This new understanding of our biology sheds a whole new light on how we should be living our lives and the process of healing. We cannot ignore the significance of this in regard to the transgenerational atmosphere we have discussed and the impact it could have on the health within a family.

We can consider if there is still a role for conventional medicine if we can do so much with our mind. Dawson Church feels that there is still a place for allopathic medicine, but there are diseases that are more likely to respond to epigenetic style treatments, harnessing that mind body connection, such as degenerative disease, cancer, autoimmune disease, viruses, in other words, the areas that traditionally have been more difficult to treat or fully understand.

Further research began to show the more psychological impacts upon brain chemistry, by examining the effects of nurturing. Dr Mosch Szyf discovered in his work with rats, that those that were very attentive to their young, grooming and caring for them had calmer less fearful offspring, the contented rats were then shown to have different brain chemistry to those who had been neglected. This of course can then be very relatable to the human condition.

The nurturing we receive and the messages we pick up when we are young will influence how we develop as adults. If we fast forward from these early enquiries into our genes, there are more recent studies that evidence for example that eight hours of mindful meditation can alter vital gene function.

There is so much research available now that clearly signpost that our belief's influence our physical and mental well-being. Interestingly for the work we are considering, Lipton argues that behavioural epigenetics get passed down through the generations. He also sites that the support an individual who has experienced trauma receives at the time immediately after the event and into recovery will significantly influence how they cope in their day to day lives and affect the long-term impact of it.

When examining the situation for my grandmother and father, there was no suitable support and they found themselves trapped in a climate of notoriety and shame which they then, it seems, unintentionally passed down the line.

One of the worrying things that came along with the understanding of genetics back in the 1950s was the belief that if we were born with a particular gene, we were trapped by it, we had no hope but be a hostage to our genes, we had to submit to that reality. The wonderful thing about epigenetics is that it gives us liberty again, we can begin to control our own destiny. I have seen this often in my therapy room with overweight people who will simply bow their heads and say they have the fat gene, everyone in their family is fat, questioning whether they can change.

I feel there is a bit of nature and nurture going on here, as in such families there is often an unhealthy relationship with food, using it as a reward, as something to soothe when upset, so they are essentially switching on that gene via their behaviour. I then see these people who have submitted to that hand of fate fight back and change their lives and many cases shining a light of hope into their family, a family where there will also be some other issues, that have yet been handed down for generations, someone needs to call a halt to that inheritance. How liberating as Church says that we can, instead of relying on a laboratory to make changes to genes, be our own genetic engineer, make our own changes through the power of our thoughts.

Did my father and grandmother get Parkinson's disease because they felt they deserved punishment for not stopping that great tragedy? Could I have believed myself into symptoms that are experienced by people with Parkinson's disease as my father was no longer here to carry the family punishment.

Perhaps I have been passed the genes associated with Parkinson's from my father, as there are genes that are considered linked to the disease, though there is, as yet no known definitive cause for the disease. This DNA distortion could of course not be the case from my grandmother to my father as he was already born when they experienced the trauma, but my father on to me, perhaps. He did show a physical expression of the trauma when it happened as he developed severe alopecia which lasted for some time, though I always knew him with a full head of hair.

After asking this question I came across some research about epigenetic mechanisms and transgenerational trauma and it states that though there is evidence within animals that trauma can be passed on through epigenetic mechanisms, there has not been enough research yet around the impacts on humans.

They raise concern about the irresponsible approach of some populist media writing scare mongering articles about the impact of trauma, citing headlines saying you can get PTSD from your ancestors. We can acknowledge that this information needs to be handled with care, but there is some evidence of epigenetic changes in analysis of holocaust survivors and interestingly there were differences noted depending on whether it was a male or female antecedent.

Unfortunately, a lot of the work around epigenetics and transgenerational trauma is still anecdotal, it is however conceded that we cannot ignore the possibility of the encoding of the trauma within the parent and that this somehow can be passed on biologically at the point of conception.

With that acknowledged, I am still inclined to think that the psychological impact of the behaviours of the parent may lead one to affect one's own biology rather than it be a biological imprint. Though I am looking at my own situation in my understanding of this and some of the clients I have worked with, this feels a far more optimistic view as if we have created something then we have a chance to alter it. I come back to my reference to the placebo affect versus the nocebo affect, we could, with the right approach change. If it is a biological inheritance, then we are rather stuck with it and can only impact on the psychological inheritance.

I must concur with Dezső Németh in the reflections section in *Transgenerational Trauma and Therapy* that there needs to be much more research into how this learning which comes from the trauma is passed through the generations. I was very surprised at the limited amount of material available, as within my client work, I regularly encounter cases where there is clearly a problem within a family that can be traced into the distant past.

We will examine a bit more regarding the theory of the impact of trauma through things like inherited loyalty and parental attachment when we look at how to use this therapeutically in the following chapters of this book.

Chapter fourteen

We have looked at the version of this family secret that I grew up with and my perceived impact of this on the whole family and found out the true story, then considered from an objective point of view how trauma might impact upon a family. So now let us examine how we can create change. For me, the writing, and investigations have been therapeutic in themselves, to finally shine a light on fact rather than guesswork, no longer hiding from the impact of what happened. If you have a family secret it may help you to write it all down, even if you are the only audience for it. We process and gain perspective by putting words upon the page.

I feel surprisingly liberated and more able to talk about it, dropping the shame that had been given to me. After all it is not my shame, but I always felt somehow tarnished by what had happened long before I was born. When I wrote the story in part one, I did it still wondering if I had a right to feel affected by this story, it was my father and grandmother's story, I am just the postscript, or so I thought.

Whilst researching for the second part of the book, I realised I did have a right to be affected by it and I also had a right to tell my story. The most powerful influence upon me was not an academic tome but a book written by someone who had experienced trauma in her family, it had so much more meaning for me when I read the echoes of my own feelings reflected in Emily Wanderer Cohen's book, a book I have mentioned earlier in this work.

Cohen discussed with a friend that surely the story belonged to her mother, it was she who had suffered, her friend challenged her about all the ways her mother's experience had impacted on her own life and the acceptance gradually came, she had a right to feel affected by it, just as I had a right to acknowledge I had been affected by what had happened in my family.

Cohen's story is full of secrecy combined with the need to find out what is real within it, so different in some ways from what she had thought. She found her therapy in the telling of her story and that of her mother, in finding the truth and no longer hiding from that truth. This all resonated with me, though our experiences are very different. We can see the ingredients for transgenerational trauma that we share in secrets, silence, and shame. The power of storytelling is hopefully woven through this book, and perhaps can help others to shine a light on their own story.

Many books on various areas of therapy are filled with case studies and intellectual analysis, here I am giving one big case study. I wanted to give a bit more detail in my book about how I approached my healing, to be transparent about my approach to therapy and to provide a journey through the tools that have been used in addition to the writing and research, many of which were developed with previous clients and are taken from a range of interventions.

The concepts here are applicable to people experiencing trauma within their family. It does not need to be a similar cause; the trauma is the wound whatever the cause and the process of healing and change can be very similar. I describe the therapeutic process I have used and then relate my response to it. It has been pointed out to me that this is quite an exposing thing for a therapist to do, interestingly Cohen too relates to a feeling of being exposed through her work, but I think it is important to be open as it can help others to begin their journey to healing.

We all have different points in our lives where something happens that can trigger change. My father's death allowed me to finally delve into this story, one I did not want to hide anymore, and I hope to be refreshingly honest about this process. As therapists, we can help others, but we may also at some point need to address something within ourselves.

We can notice by looking at my story, that if you do not tell an adolescent or young adult the full information at an appropriate time about family information or heritage, they will fill in the gaps, adding to what small truths they are given and over time the two coalesce together to become an accepted truth. We must consider that any distortions that are created in the story could be more damaging than the truth. I have yet to discover whether my creations within the story have helped or hindered me, but I feel the truth should always be at the forefront of any processing of trauma or it cannot be effectively healed, as we cannot heal shadows, we can only address truths, however uncomfortable they may be.

My teenage identification with the fear of committing suicide in my sleep that sounds ridiculous to my adult self, was however very real to me then and it frightened me. I feel now that I know the whole story, or as much as I can now find, that this might not have happened if I had known the full story. My aunt's actions seem linked to post-natal and pre-natal depression, had I known this earlier in my life, so much of my young uncertainties would have been removed. Had my mother known the full story, she may have been less concerned about me too and I would not have picked up so much fear within the family home. The truth is easier to process and deal with than a myth. I am no longer fighting shadows.

When I set out on this journey, I was experiencing neurological symptoms, which I had always seen as somehow connected to this trauma when my grandmother and father experienced them. I cannot know if this has affected me too, but as the information has unfolded and I have been reflecting upon the tragedy, I see there have been psychological impacts upon me, as well as potentially some physical symptoms.

Chapter fifteen

I have already mentioned that this sudden night-time awakening and the accompanying confusion had worsened, this has been the most challenging symptom. Though it can be a classic Parkinson's symptom to struggle to awaken fully from the dream state, these experiences can affect anyone, but particularly people affected by fear. It accompanies being very active/restless in sleep and having nightmares.

I had begun delaying going to bed to avoid what inevitably lay ahead of me and I was getting steadily more and more tired. It also seemed that the more tired I was the worse the disturbances became. I asked myself what I would do for a client with similar problems.

I would recommend self-hypnosis or autosuggestion just before sleep, as originally developed from the work of Emile Coue, which he defines as a way of influencing the body through the power of imagination.

So, this is the process I adopted: I chose a cue

word for the work, my cue word was mountain. I started by saying the word and closing my eyes, at first seeing images of a mountain to take my mind away from its usual busy thoughts. I then worked on a body relaxation, repeated phrases like my limbs are tired and heavy, tired and relaxed and they just do not want to work, I am tired and sleepy, sleepier and sleepier. I worked on relaxing my muscles from the top of my head right down to my feet, building in some suggestions about my eyelids being heavy too and they just want to stay closed. Thus, combining some mindful body relaxation with a classic eye-closure technique used throughout hypnosis, which can be easily worked with by oneself. This eye closure method was developed by David Elman and Milton Erickson from the early work of James Braid in the 19th Century.

When I was really relaxed and felt heavy in my body, unable or unwilling to move, I knew I had done what we call 'bypassed my critical faculty' and I would accept the words I would now use. I then said my cue word a second time and repeated three mantras, 'I will not sleepwalk', 'I will awaken fully from a dream' and 'My dreams will be peaceful'. I said each of these slowly with real focussed attention ten times. To end the session, I said the cue word again. This may sound very simplistic, using affirmations in a relaxed state, but I have had great success with clients using such bedtime techniques.

The first time I tried it I fell asleep earlier than I had been doing and though I awoke from a dream in the night, I did not jump out of my bed as I often do. I realised I had been dreaming straight away, did not find myself stuck in a confused limbo land in my dreams and could fully awaken. As I was not distressed from the confusion I would normally experience. I was able to fall quite quickly back to sleep, the dream state was also less plagued by nightmare. My prescription for myself was to repeat this process every night for about a week and then see if I had altered the pattern enough, to just go straight to sleep.

I had begun to be so desperate about these disturbances as I did not know how to pull myself out of the sleep state without assistance. If you have not experienced this, it must be rather hard to understand what is so disturbing about it. You feel so confused and cannot find firm ground in reality, you question yourself, try to trace through what has happened, almost at war with yourself, trying to seek reality until the moment when the fog finally clears and you know who you are and where you are again, falling back into bed in relief. It can be disturbing for anyone sleeping beside you as you suddenly jump up startling them. The first time they might think something awful has happened until they realise you are not making sense; you argue with them and gradually you again find your way back to reality.

If someone is in the room with me, I can easily be reassured by being told I am stuck in a dream state. Maintaining this plan of self-hypnosis each night I have succeeded in keeping these disturbances at bay.

Having dealt with this primary symptom I wanted to examine some of the learning, feelings and patterns that might be acquired in a generational trauma situation.

Chapter sixteen

WHAT WE LEARN IN THE TRANSGENERATIONAL ATMOSPHERE

I want to examine now some of the themes that come out of the transgenerational atmosphere and how they can manifest. These may resonate with anyone who has had trauma within their family in the past or present.

GUILT

One of the key issues in a family with trauma is guilt, guilt at not preventing something happening, guilt at being a survivor, guilt at being relieved it was not you who had suffered, guilt at being relieved that a situation has passed. Those most affected by the event will transmit their feelings of guilt into the family and then it can become a learned pattern for others.

Alternatively, sometimes a family member will take on guilt for another who is not owning, or has never addressed their own guilt. Indra Torsten

Preiss addresses this in his work on family constellation therapy.

My grandparents and father had tangible guilt for not understanding how bad things were for my aunt, for not saving her and the children, which then affected their behaviours. They very quickly apologised in any situation when blame was not theirs to take and took responsibility for all the woes of the world. It used to frustrate me how my father was too ready to see someone else's point of view, rather than standing up and fighting for himself, yet I took that on, I copied him.

I realise that in the past I had jumped very quickly into the position of apology and responsibility. I have felt guilty about hurting someone's feelings even if they are in the wrong, I felt I had to appease and make everything alright, so I have squeezed myself into any position to keep other people happy. I was taught to put my needs last until I began my own therapeutic journey some years ago, I eventually started to see where I had some rights in a situation.

I had not made any enquiry as to where all my guilt came from until now. Guilt needs to be addressed at its source, then it can be gifted back to our ancestors, and we can heal at a deeper level. I lived in an atmosphere of guilt without having a clear understanding of what was wrong, what I had done. This was especially hard for a small child to understand and of course that child grew up, carrying the guilt with her.

JUDGEMENT AND PUNISHMENT

Judgement will often accompany trauma, the fear of what the outside world thinks of us, how does it judge us, will others think we are complicit in the suffering our family has experienced. Judgement is closely aligned with guilt. In my family that judgement led to guilt and then, as they were so steeped in the Catholic Church, punishment followed on.

If we think of any parent who feels they have failed to protect their child from rape, abduction or suicide, there will be a fear of judgement from the outside world, then guilt and then the need to atone, what can they do to make good, to recompense. I think my father and grandmother felt they had been judged for letting my aunt and the children down and that the Parkinson's was their just punishment, they accepted it stoically. I learned that we deserved to be punished for our sins.

I learned that even if you make a mistake that is not a deliberately bad act, you will be punished for it, you will have to recompense, you must pay a price and that price may be your health.

It was only when I reflected upon this, I realised just how this had manifested in my life more than I had realised. When I was thirty-four, I had a partner who was very mentally unwell and I tried to support them, but it became impossible, I felt I had to save myself from the relationship and ended it after five years of struggle, an action deemed long overdue by my friends who had watched me suffer.

I only stayed due to a sense of responsibility for someone mentally unwell, I had to make sacrifices for them. I had learned that I had to put myself second as I was mentally strong, for if my grandmother had said yes and allowed my aunt and her children to live with her, they might have survived. I was going to save this one!

After I left, my partner took an overdose and went into respiratory arrest, they were on a life support machine for two days and thankfully survived. My father broke down weeping when he heard. I have a vivid image in my mind of him crying sitting in a chair at the top of the stairs unable to move up or down, just sobbing. I felt I had to protect him from being exposed to such pain. I struggled with my guilt at his distress, my partner's action and blamed myself for not handling things better and became very seriously ill with encephalitis. This left me with some sight problems that took many years to improve, and I still battle with headaches to this day, what an exceptional punishment.

I had thought maybe the stress of the experience had made me ill, I had not considered the role of the guilt until now, guilt at not preventing a suicide, guilt at leaving, very close to my family story though not as extreme. Now I understand this too, I can make peace with it.

The link between my family experience and my own may seem obvious from the outside, the view was very different from the inside! This ex-partner died three years ago, not from their own hand but a rather odd complication from an illness, just two weeks after I got married to my now stable lovely partner. I had to be careful not to fall into that pit of responsibility again, I could not have changed their life, only they could, and they chose not to.

RESPONSIBILITY

If we become overprotective due to tragedy within a family, then we can take on too much responsibility for others, we can have poor boundaries and not allow individuals to grow into themselves, we will look further at boundaries later on. I learned I had to look after others as you can see from my story above, it was my responsibility because I was strong and no matter how badly someone behaved, I learned that I had to accept it. Someone once said to me I had a high tolerance for bad behaviour. I am glad to say that I have set my tolerance to a realistic level now, but in the past, I am sure I was given this sense of responsibility. I returned to the relationship with the partner who attempted suicide and it was a further seven years before I ended it for good.

I wonder in how many ways this sense of responsibility for others might filter into one's life from something buried deep in the family past. If this sense of people pleasing or constantly putting your own needs second resonates with you, it is time to start to take care of you and look for the origins of this behaviour and make peace with it.

SHAME

Shame accompanies many traumas, shame at not being able to prevent it, shame at not coping with it, shame at being seen to be weak, shame at being thought complicit. Shame is interesting as it has an important role in our survival, it evolved as part of our instinct to survive as in early mankind we needed to belong to a group, or community to remain safe. If we do something that brings shame upon us, we are at risk of being expelled from the group so we will go to great lengths to avoid shame. This is relevant to modern society too, the need to belong is a powerful one, it can lead people to denounce others and compromise themselves just to stay with the in crowd.

We see this so clearly in children's behaviours at school. So, it is the fear of shame that can prevent us from doing things that will lead to expulsion from the group, but shame can be thrust upon us by others, and this is out of our control. Though the intent of shame is a positive one the outcome is clearly a negative one.

I learned shame in relation to my aunt, it felt to me this was why we could not talk about it, though I do appreciate the family may also have felt too much pain to discuss it. The act of my aunt affected the reputation of the family and could be seen to put it at risk. People can be very judgemental and blame the upbringing of those who commit crimes, so a victim of their judgement can quickly become outcast.

The publicity that surrounded the tragedy would undoubtedly have had fed that feeling of family shame, it must have felt a very public and exposing experience which carried with it fears of judgement from friends, family and the wider public. I absorbed the family shame unconsciously, having absorbed this and with the limited information I had, I had not been able to connect with my aunt other than in negative ways.

Through this process of healing, I want to connect with her and see her in my mind as she was before the tragedy. My father and grandmother had a vision of her other than this suicidal child murderer. I want a sense of her as other than this too, and this has begun, it is helping me to let go of the shame and perhaps has given me an awareness of shame that has filtered into my life in other ways that I am only just beginning to understand. We must be careful not to carry shame for others and if we feel shame, we should examine it carefully to see if it really belongs to us.

If we learn to take on the mantle of shame at an early age, we become quick to judge ourselves too. The problem with inherited shame is that you were not in a position to alter the outcome of events, so you need to find a way to heal from someone else's mistake, to make your peace with that mistake and if you do not have all the information, it will be harder to achieve this acceptance.

DISSOCIATION AND REJECTION

If a family has experienced a lot of pain, a coping strategy is to dissociate from their emotions, this is part of the stress response and creates protection through distance from feeling. If a family member is regularly dissociating, as with all learning, this can be absorbed by other members who may go on to develop patterns of breaking relationships before they are at risk of being hurt or just not allowing anyone to get too close. I learned to shut out my cousins because it was too painful to remember them, it was easier to reject all thought of them.

I have been aware of a pattern in the past of shutting down on people as a form of protection in this way, so I need to welcome my cousins into my consciousness, I feel that for me this will help to address this once and for all.

BLAME

Blame is often an expression of inner pain and discomfort, as Brene Brown points out in her work. Clearly this is the case in my family but also guilt can often lead to blame; it is easier to blame others than take responsibility for our own actions or our role in what has happened. In my family I think there was a lot of blame levelled at my uncle, I learned to blame my uncle for his role in the story and never consider apportioning blame to my grandparents or father. Shame can lead to blame, as the family is affected by an individual's action. Taking on their shame, they then project their blame outwards. If we jump too quickly towards blame it can be a way to avoid taking responsibility for ourselves.

I need to look at my family situation, make peace with my uncle and let go of blame, shame, and guilt that I may have absorbed along the way, without any conscious understanding of these learnings I was taking on. I also learned some blame of my aunt for taking my cousins away, without knowing what must have been going on for her to take such drastic action.

Shame, blame, judgement, and guilt are the features of trauma of all kinds, these feelings will be familiar to anyone who has experienced it.

Whether it is inherited trauma, or the trauma is directly experienced, the healing processes can be very similar irrespective of how the learnings have been acquired.

HOW TO CHALLENGE THESE LEARNINGS

There is a simple technique that can be used to begin to acknowledge these learnings and begin the process of letting them go, it involves a simple visualisation. In this exercise you are sending a message into the subconscious that you do not want to act out these behaviours anymore, this becomes the catalyst of change and a new awareness. I used this process to reinforce some change I had already worked upon, given the new knowledge I felt I needed to revisit it.

Imagine you are walking into a walled garden, through the gate in the wall, click it shut behind you and look around. See the green of the grass, freshly cut, flowers and shrubs and maybe just maybe you had overlooked the trees in the garden, hearing their leaves rustle and the birdsong. The sun is warm against your skin, take in the colours of nature you can see around you, in the flowers and shrubs, can you smell them I wonder, taking your time to absorb the scene around you and when you are ready, head over towards the trees, there is somewhere to sit beneath a tree, perhaps a bench or deckchair or maybe you need to hunker down and lean your back against the trunk of the tree.

See the patterns on the ground created by the shadows of the branches and the sunlight dappling down through those branches. Then look up and see the leaves moving, branches swaying slightly in a gentle breeze, as you watch, a small leaf detaches itself and begins to spin and dance in the air, spinning and twisting down towards the ground. Watching this helps you to relax your mind and your body as you watch its journey on down towards the ground.

In this more relaxed state, you glance around the garden spread out in front of you, letting your eyes roam and drift and then some smoke rising in the distance catches your eye, it must be a bonfire, you are going to investigate. So, rise from your place beneath the tree and wend your way through the garden to find the fire. You may need to cut across the lawn or follow some small gravel paths carving a way through the shrubs, however you get there, find your way to the bonfire. Then, there it is in front of you, you see the flames dance and leap, the colours within the flames, blues, purples, reds, and yellows, watching them ripple and move, perhaps hearing the snap and pop of the fire or you may notice the smell of the woodsmoke.

Nearby on the ground you see what looks like a pack of playing cards and you bend down to pick them up, but they are cards with single words written upon them, words that describe feelings.

Shuffle through and find those that you most relate to but would like to release, words like blame, shame, guilt, judgement, there may be images that accompany the words, I am not sure as they are your cards.

It may be interesting to shuffle them and cut the deck and see what word is there, if you are struggling with working out the key ones you want to let go of today that may be the best thing to do. The word you find will be important for you to release today. When you have selected your card or cards, place the remainder on the ground and either scrunch up or tear up the ones you want to release and throw them into the heart of the fire. You have identified what you need to let go of and now you will remember these feeling have no part in your life, as you watch the paper burn, char and dissolve into ash and dust. This brings the experience to a close, take some time to orientate yourself back to awareness of where you are in space and time.

Not everyone can visualise things well, it does not matter how clearly you experience the images, just working with the idea of it is important, you may wish to focus on different senses to help you engage with the process more. You can do this exercise as often as you need to, to address these feelings that have been gifted to you that you do not wish to carry around with you anymore. Acknowledging what needs to change is the first step on that journey, working with it in this way engages your creative powers to imagine change and begin the process of making it your reality.

Chapter seventeen

These emotions, patterns and responses creating the atmosphere we have discussed can be traced partly to an inherited loyalty, a family loyalty that many of us have drummed into us. Belonging to our family has a price tag attached to it, we fit into a position given to us within the family and fulfilling that role is the price of belonging. Ivan Boszormenyi-Nagy in his article *Loyalty implications of the transference model* talks of how we can collude unconsciously to fulfil a role within the family, and he specifically relates this to sickness at one point and I feel this concept has great relevance for me and for so many of my clients.

Nagy speaks of 'obligations' to the family and we can consider what those family obligations will lead us to believe and do. It is fascinating how these obligations can insidiously creep in under our radar as they are absorbed unconsciously, so it is much harder to challenge them. I have used a metaphor to treat unconscious loyalty, which leads us to take on the issues of our ancestors, to cut through the transference, to question the loyalty and develop individual values and beliefs. I will outline this metaphor later.

A trauma experience within a family can alter and change the internal patterns within that family and the responses. These changes are not decided consciously, that is why we need to be working with the unconscious to change/alter those obligations and one of the best ways to do this is with metaphors. Let's remind ourselves here that when the ideas of consciousness, subconscious and unconscious were developed, the perception was that around 90 per cent of our habits and behaviours were unconscious. There is a school of thought now that believes that even that small 10 per cent conscious control is an illusion.

Most of the therapeutic work that follows has been done within the trance state as in this state we can access the subconscious mind. If we think about the dream state, our dreams are so vivid and real, sometimes the feelings they create whether good or bad stay with us for days or even weeks. For example, you can have a dream about your partner betraying you and when you wake up and see them sleeping peacefully beside you, you can feel real anger towards them that stays with you for a while, even though they have done nothing to hurt you. The memory of the dream itself can stay forever with us, but it is the associated feelings I am interested in.

When we are working in trance we are working with the subconscious and these ideas explored this way are more vivid, real, and intense. Though self-hypnosis can be a powerful tool, I would not recommend using it for issues relating to trauma, someone needs to be there to support and steer the individual through the process.

A trance state is something each of us experiences every day; it is a completely natural state, one that happens at least twice a day. When you first wake up in the morning and you have not opened your eyes yet, you are just becoming conscious, you are aware of sound, such as perhaps birds singing outside but cannot quite bring yourself to open your eyes yet, you feel cosy and comfortable and unaffected by troubles and demands of your daily life, this is a trance state. When you are just drifting off to sleep at night, we feel the same, drowsy, and comfortable, we are still slightly conscious but unaffected by an active mind, this is a trance state.

We also drift into a trance state at different times during the day, less deep perhaps but nonetheless a trance state. For example; when you have driven along the motorway and you suddenly realise that you have passed junction turn offs and had not noticed; you have finished all the washing up but do not remember doing it; when you are playing an instrument and it feels like the instrument is almost playing itself, you become so focused and the outside world disappears; when you are doing something creative like painting or maybe even something active like dancing or repetitive exercise, in all these situations we can zone out and drift into a trance state. There is a kind of music labelled as trance, one that is repetitive and lulls you into a zone where nothing outside the experience matters and maybe this concept can help us understand the trance.

When we work within the trance state, the conscious mind has gone partly off duty, it is there but not in controlling mode. We bypass the critical faculty of the mind and can work meaningfully with change. We can access the subconscious to affect a change, it is like the hard drive on your computer with a faulty programme that we need to work on and repair, or to use an older metaphor, it is a pre-recorded tape that needs recording over.

Chapter eighteen

HEALING INHERITED TRAUMA/LOYALTY WITH METAPHOR

Metaphor is a powerful way to work with the unconscious as it slips past our defences. I often compare it to the way we hide medicine for a pet within their food, the medicine lies within the story. The metaphor helps us to connect two sets of ideas, comparing two things with similar traits and they are familiar to us as a means of communicating concepts. When we say I can see the light at the end of the tunnel, it has so much more power than simply saying things are going to get better. The visual imagery enforces the idea for us and within metaphor we can also employ more poetic language, rhythm and meter which can help lull the mind into acceptance.

We are used to learning from parables and fables in childhood and our ancestors would have sat around fires listening to stories all of which had meaning for the listener. We can harness this familiarity and human desire to listen to a story to elicit change. When we use metaphors in a therapeutic way, we are looking for that eureka moment of understanding when the idea behind the story clicks into place and the message comes home. In Rubin Battino's book *Metaphoria* he suggests that all kinds of story and day-dreams allow us a safe way to explore new ideas. I have created a range of metaphors for therapeutic use in my book 'The Healing Metaphor'

The metaphor I am using here, was devised by Maureen Williams who has been guiding me through this process, I have developed it a little and it was delivered within a trance state.

THE COAT

Your grandmother wove a coat for your father, she did it with great love and care and within the making of the coat she wove all the learnings from her own life to prepare him, so he had a map to show him the way and from time to time she would repair a small hole here or a snagged thread there and she would bring in new threads, new learnings and experiences over the years. The coat was treasured by your father as a special gift and he kept it safely to hand on to you, as part of your inheritance.

When your grandmother became too old and frail to care for that coat for him, he began to add his own threads, make his own additions to the special family coat, perhaps you can imagine the colour, shape and style of this well-tended, loved, and treasured coat. You have looked at the coat over the years and considered the time it will be yours, yours to tend and keep safe and learn from, this magical ancestral coat.

So your time comes, your father is too old to take care of the coat as he does not go outside much anymore, so now it is yours and you, with great pride you take the coat in your hands, a bit surprised at first by the weight of it and you put your arms into the sleeves and you shrug it on, pulling it over your shoulders, straight away you feel weighed down by it, then over time you feel smothered by it and you begin to resent carrying the coat that you had waited all these years to be yours. You drag it around with you, it is too hot in the summer and gets waterlogged and even heavier in the winter, yet it is your gift from the family, you must be loyal to the family, and keep dragging around this old, now outmoded, worn-out, worn-down coat. Is it really the right coat for these times I wonder? Is it the right coat for you now?

If it were not so heavy, not such a burden you could perhaps keep carrying the coat, maybe, just maybe you can make some changes to the coat. You lay the coat out on a table in front of you and carefully, attentively you begin to unpick some of the stitching on the coat, and you find to your surprise there are some stones sewn into the lining of the coat and you take them out one by one. There may be some words written on the stones. If there are, notice noticing the words as you cast each stone away, one by one, you cast them away and you feel around the lining of the coat to make sure every last stone is gone. I wonder if you notice already feeling a relief at getting rid of those stones in the coat and now you can take some new threads and weave your own new learnings into that coat.

I wonder what colours you will use to brighten up that coat, to change and adapt that coat to make it yours, to make it represent your story not theirs, to make the changes that you need, to address the fact that your life is not their life. You are an individual, it does not mean you do not respect the past and those that went before you, but you can assess now what part of the learnings you want to keep and what you want to change. So, use the material that is there to create your own coat, new from old, a blending, a developing, creating your own coat, writing your own story, and when you have placed that last stitch and I am giving you a few minutes now for you to do what you need to do.

Think about it for a couple of minutes. Now your work is complete you can lift that coat up, pull it on and see how it fits, a better fit now and so much lighter. You can fit layers under it for those cold winter days, yet it is light enough for a mild day and it is so tailored to fit you it is like an extension of your own skin, supple and sleek and easy to wear. See it clearly in your mind's eye. Now you have changed the coat, you have changed the story, you cut the coat from the same cloth, so you have not broken your loyalty to the coat, but you have made it yours now and it is the right fit, the right weight, what a relief. I wonder if you can feel the change yet, the lightness, the freedom from other people's stories, that were not your story. You have let it go now. Let the past go now but kept faith with your family too, you feel lighter, freer, and easier, what a relief.

Chapter nineteen

MERGING

In Mark Wolynn's book, *It Didn't start With You*, he looks at the idea of merging with a parent. There is so much focus in therapy on interrupted and broken connections with parents but merging and becoming too close can be equally damaging. Wolynn argues that this merging often occurs when a parent seems vulnerable or hurt and the child wants to fix the problem, help the parent, so they, without conscious choice, take on the problem of the parent.

Wolynn suggests that if a child is busy managing the parents' problem, they become stuck in giving mode and can get caught up in patterns of struggling to receive. This also raises the question of whether the merged child has the capacity to create proper boundaries in future relationships of all kinds.

These issues are echoed in a paper in the JCN on preventing transgenerational trauma. One of the key issues raised is that of parental attachment. Where a parent has experienced trauma, it is acknowledged that this can lead to lifelong trauma for the child and a potentiality to experience other traumas. The main treatment proposed is to help the parent resolve their trauma and deal with the attachment issues. In my case it is too late to deal with my father's trauma, but I feel the attachment issues can be addressed even though my father is no longer alive.

As a child I was not consciously aware of my father's pain, but I must have sensed it. I have already explained the intensity of my relationship with him, I feel my bond with him was so strong that I wanted to help him, realising this was a poignant moment for me. This led in my case to my father's guilt becoming my guilt, then maybe his punishment became my punishment.

Separation needs to happen for me to release the guilt, acknowledge it is not mine, so that I no longer need to experience the punishment. As my father is now dead, his punishment is perceptibly over anyway, debt paid, so this needs to be acknowledged too as part of the separation process.

Tihamér Bahó and Katalin Zana in their book which I have already mentioned, *Transgenerational Trauma and Therapy*, describe dealing with this merging by creating a 'me-identity' rather than a 'we-identity'. They, like Wolynn, stress the importance of the separation, or differentiation, otherwise a person is responding not to the present but a past that is not even theirs. They advise this should only be attempted when and if someone has a strong enough sense of self before tackling the separation. They need to have established security before the perceived security of the we-identity is taken away, as the individual has only recognised the security benefits and not the harm of the lack of self-actualisation.

The parent can fear the loss of identity that they have placed within their child, so there can be resistance from both sides at this concept of separation. In my case I know I have a strong sense of self and am not concerned that I cannot cope with the separation, especially as I have already gone through my father's death and obviously, I do not have to negotiate his resistance.

By no longer hiding the trauma away and bringing it into my consciousness and more significantly breaking the promise to my father that I would never look for the inquest, I have already begun to assert myself, my needs. I have begun to break away from my father through seeing my need to seek the truth as more significant than his wish for me to leave it well alone.

This is a powerful step forward and shows to me clearly that I can make that break now. The insight comes to me that as I find it possible to assert my needs over my father's needs, I can apply this to other situations where I may still subjugate my own needs for another's, that learned childhood pattern to comply rather than upset someone who is fragile.

I cannot stress enough what a powerful realisation this has been. I have seen this process in others, it is so interesting to experience it from the inside. It is only through doing this work that I even realised I had merged with my father, though people had observed our closeness, I always saw this as something to be proud of, and not in any way damaging to me. So onward now towards the separation process.

One way we do this kind of separation within hypnotherapy comes from Neuro Linguistic Programming (NLP) and is called cutting the ties. We use this often for someone who needs to cut from their attachment to a previous partner, but the prospect of doing this for my father fills me with resistance, which makes it more important that I do follow through this process.

RESOURCE STATE

Before doing work that could trigger an emotional reaction, known as an abreaction, it is important to create a positive resource state to reconnect to in case the therapeutic process becomes upsetting. I create a resource state with all my clients as part of a first session. This usually involves visualising within a trance state a memory with a good feeling, recreating an experience they enjoy doing and then imagining a place in nature that they like. Once they have gone through this process, they anchor the positive feeling by touching the thumb and forefinger together. This enables them to reconnect to those good feelings whenever they feel the need to do so, when they need to access a safe place. In the situation I am looking to tackle within my own therapeutic process, I feel I cannot connect to any previous resource states that I have created, as they usually involve a place I associate with my childhood and my father, this would be counterproductive for the work we are doing here.

It is important when creating a resource state to make sure it has no links to the issue you are working with, for example an alcoholic cannot be imagining a time out drinking with friends although it has a good feeling for them.

When I looked at creating a new resource state, I felt resistance at abandoning the place I had always retreated to in my mind. The resistance signalled the importance of finding the new space. To help with this I began to look at photos of travels in recent years as the photo would help enhance this new image for me, especially as I was replacing something very entrenched in my mind. At first, I was drawn to images of Ireland but that linked me strongly to my mother's family. I needed to find something fresher, somewhere I could make my own, away from my family.

I found a picture of a visit to Arthur's Seat in

Edinburgh. Edinburgh is my favourite city; it is a place I see as unconnected to my family despite having some Scottish roots. I love the mountains above the city, it gives you the best of both worlds, combining nature with civilisation. I decided that I had found my place and I had a memory to put with it of a warm October day when I climbed up on the rocks. I began to imagine, to take myself right back there to that moment, the sky is the most incredible azure blue, not a cloud anywhere, just this stretch of blue more suited to a July day in the Mediterranean than October in Edinburgh. I am wrapped up for the cold, but as I begin to walk up the tarmac path at the bottom of the climb up to the craggy summit I begin to sweat, so I take off my coat and tie it around my waist and made my way up the slope, rising into a climb rather than a stroll. There is the mix of green grass, yellow gorse, purple heather, and the intermittent protrusions of rock as the climb became steeper and steeper, hard to believe I am in the heart of a city, with a gin making business nestling just at the start of the climb.

I smell an aroma of grasses that is very specific to Scotland for me, breathing in this fresh smell, feeling the sun warm upon my skin, and feeling the pull in my calves as I strain my body pushing on higher and higher. I stop halfway up, turn around and look back seeing the city spread out below me on one side, the spires of St Giles, the sweep of the buttress of the castle, the high rises here and there and the water of the Firth of Forth stretching along for miles and miles at the edge of the city. Then, I return to the climb, the rocks rare really craggy and uneven, reflecting their volcanic origins, not so hard to believe now this is the site of an old volcano, despite the other tourists scrambling up both behind and in front of me, the rhythm of the walk takes me inwards, and I can zone out from them and just engage with the land.

As I near the top I find a crag that no one else has reached creating a cleft that I can sit in, perching like an eagle in its nest from up high and look out at the land spread out before me. It is one of those perfect moments, I am there, up there, breathing in the fresh grass filled air, the warmth soaks into my limbs, the sun on my upturned face, that blue sky, such an incredible blue that remains etched in my mind. I feel a surge of contentment up here, in a fanciful way I feel a link to my Scottish ancestors, the Robertson clan, not in any complicated way, just a comforting sense of belonging in this land, I feel peaceful, cradled and safe high up here in this old volcanic mass, and I can take that with me wherever I go, this moment, this place, I can retreat here in my mind. I anchor this image and this specific moment in time by placing my thumb and forefinger together.

All I have to do if I need to, is press my finger and thumb together at any time and I will evoke the good feelings again, the feelings have been saved in my body memory, which I may need to do as my therapeutic journey progresses.

Once I had created the resource state, I moved into cutting that connection.

CUTTING THE CONNECTION

Imagine you are in a field of wheat, you can see the heads of corn waving in the breeze, the sky is blue above you, you are not alone, your father is with you, as you remember him as a young man, remember how you used to walk together through the fields and sit in the dunes and he would read to you, that is how you see him now. *I took some time before starting this process to focus on a photograph so this image could be very clear for me and so it is, walking through the corn field smiling together, I see it clearly.*

Eventually you reach some flattened down corn in the shape of a circle, a corn circle and next to it is another circle, two large circles of pressed down corn, making a giant figure of eight before you. Now you know what you need to do. Your father walks across the corn to stand in one circle whilst you make your way to the other, you stand facing each other and something joins you stretching across the two circles, in this case it is a piece of red ribbon, it is tied around my waist with a complex series of knots and it stretches across my circles, hanging low to the ground and it is wrapped around my father's waist too, also tied with more than one knot. You look across and meet his eyes.

What you are going to do does not harm your relationship or feelings, it just creates autonomy, it breaks that merging, it will make you both whole and complete, not just you, this is for him too. So you need to look around on the ground for some scissors to cut that connection. *I feel the hesitation as I slip from first to third person, trying to distance myself from what I need to do, but I need to be present, I need to feel the weight of the scissors in my hand, like cutting the umbilical cord at last, and beginning to be me. I wonder what will change, not only the carrying of burdens with him or for him, but the things you felt you could never do as he would not have done them, living up to those expectations and not always quite meeting them, time to cut that connection.*

I look down at the series of knots, I place the ribbon between the blades of the scissors, and I screw my eyes shut as I cut and it is done. I still love him can feel close to him but no longer a part of him, I can allow others closer in. It is done, I did it, I look over at him, he does not look hurt. Maybe, just maybe it was a burden to him too, maybe he can rest in peace now without constantly worrying about me. I am wondering as I survey the changes in me, if he had not cut the connection with his mother, that is what added to this complex web around us, wrapping us three together, so I am breaking free of the trio we were and beginning to find just me.

I search in my mind to see how it feels for just me to be present and, surprisingly it feels good. Not an incomplete feeling but a polished up and finished feeling.

BOUNDARIES

People who have been associated with trauma may have experienced merging with the affected person or be caught in a web of family loyalty which can lead to boundary issues. We had already begun to examine this but let us look at how specifically it affects boundaries. For example, if someone is used to pacifying a troubled individual, someone they feel has a right to be upset, they are likely to give in to that person's needs, prioritising them. This behaviour is then taken into other areas of life, creating weak boundaries, this can be fed by a fear of upsetting others and an avoidance of conflict.

The individual with weak boundaries may then attract into their life people who will push at their boundaries and not take no for an answer. We often know when someone is pushing at our boundaries, as we will feel tension in our bodies and a rising resentment but feel unable to assert our needs. When finally the needs are asserted, it can be in anger or may only be negotiated through lying, such as making up a reason why you cannot do something rather than just telling the truth and saying you do not want to do it. If any of this sounds familiar to you then you may need to look at your boundaries.

Having appropriate boundaries does not mean you cannot care for other people, but it starts with beginning to prioritise the self. Many people fear this means becoming selfish, but it is not about being selfish but self-aware. We cannot care for the people in our lives if we do not care for ourselves first.

The next exercise brings an awareness that leads to creating better boundaries, boundaries that had been blurred before or sometimes even trampled all over, now they can be reset. I used this exercise after the 'cutting the ties' work to cement the change.

SETTING NEW BOUNDARIES

Imagine you are standing on a sandy beach, it is a clear bright summer's day, you may be aware of the warmth of the sun upon your skin, focus on the waves as they lap the shore, the white surf rolling up the beach and back again. Listen to the sound, the rhythm of the in and out of the sea rather like the rhythm of your breath and it relaxes you even more as you watch, listen and feel the relaxation sweeping through you, the warmth of the sun bringing a familiar drowsy feeling, perhaps you might even notice that fresh salty smell in the air rising up from the sea and the surf rides up the beach, perhaps some spray touching your skin. Now you are ready to begin. Look along the shoreline for a piece of driftwood, small enough to hold in your hand and draw upon the sand.

When you have found the right piece of wood find a wide stretch of beach, stand as centrally as you can and draw a circle around exactly where you stand, big enough to stand in but not big enough for anything else, just a centimetre or two around the edge of you. Then step outside this circle and draw another creating a ring around the first circle, draw a series of concentric circles stretching larger and wider, so that when you have finished the beach has circles within circles reducing to the first one that you drew. Then tread over the lines you have made in the sand until you reach the central circle and step inside it again.

This is your boundary, no one else can come inside this circle now as you are no longer merged but autonomous, it is as if there is a forcefield around the circle that keeps others at bay. Now imagine your parents in the circle next to you and your partner. Then assign positions for other family members, friends, and acquaintances in the other circles, some near and some far, each person has their place, their position within the boundaries you have created now. From this day on, you are separate, autonomous, protected. You no longer share other's experiences, only yours alone, you share no other's guilt, shame, judgement. You make your own judgements as you find them. Your view is your own view, from your position, from your place, it is no longer tainted or tinted by another's perspective.

I asked a hypnotherapist I trusted to work on the above material with me. She put me into trance, did the positive resource, cutting the ties, the boundaries exercise ending with the coat metaphor. What astonished me was, that I had written this material, but it felt one dimensional until I experienced it in trance. When I experienced the coat, I saw my grandmother clearly pass it to my father and I felt the learning she had woven in it and I felt the additions of my father as he took it over, it was so vivid and clear. When I opened the lining there were stones in there, labelled guilt, shame, blame, punishment, and I cast them away. I crafted a new coat, the colours clear and the cut changed, it felt like my coat, and I saw myself modelling it in the mirror and I felt in charge of my beliefs.

I had expressed that I was worried I would resist the 'cutting the ties' exercise, but when it happened, I was ready, I saw my father as a young and vibrant man which made it easier. I followed through for both of us, the need for autonomy. I then set my clear boundaries and there were times within the work where I felt I wanted to smile, I felt in control of my destiny, my beliefs, and thoughts in a way I had not felt before. I cannot find the words to express the depth of power that came from this trance experience.

THE CONVERSATION

When I had completed the separation from my father and enforced new boundaries, I felt in a position to have the conversation my father and I were never allowed to have in the past. As my father has died, I must use my imagination and creative powers to do this work, but it is never too late to do this. It is easier within a trance state, as again we bypass the critical faculty and create a more real and vivid experience.

This approach is based on the kind of 'talk to the chair' work often done within Gestalt therapy, which is intended to achieve integration. It involves having a discourse with someone in a way we would not be able to in day-to-day life, or with different aspects of the self, getting a sense of both positions. As I aim to move from a we-mentality to a me-position, the dialogue needs to happen to enforce the differentiation and gain a two-sided perspective.

This process would have been harder to do if I had not worked on the separation and boundary issues, or it would have felt like an attack on the we-self, now it is a dialogue between two perceived autonomous selves.

This dialogue form I have worked with has some inspiration drawn from work in Tristine Rainor's book *The New Diary* which includes a dialogue with someone who has died, with whom there is unfinished business. This book provides excellent guidance on ways to use a diary in a form of personal therapy. So, we are blending different therapeutic approaches to find something that can fit this kind of trauma resolution. A script follows that was worked through with a therapist.

Visualise for yourself in a comfortable room with armchairs and places to sit. How do you want to decorate this room, the walls, the floor, what are the windows like? Create a room that is light and airy, one you may know or a creation in your mind of a perfect room.

See your father sitting in the room, he is an age that seems most familiar to you, when you connected with him most and the 'you' of today sits near him. So now is your time, the time to have the conversation you never had. After you have worked through the conversation writing it down can help.

Me: I am glad we have this time, I wanted to ask you some things, some things I never felt able to ask you before and I hope we can now have this conversation without you getting upset. So why wouldn't you talk to me about it, about the loss of your sister and her family? You did not talk about any of it.

Dad: It just hurt too much, and I did not want your life to be blighted by something that happened before you were born, I wanted to protect you from it.

Me: That is just not possible though, the only way you could have done that is to have never told me they had existed and that would have meant grandma denying her daughter and never showing the picture. I was bound to be inquisitive about it with that picture always there.

Dad: I wanted to pretend it had not happened, I did not want to relive it by talking about it and I really believed you would accept what I told you and leave it be, after all you did not know them.

Me: They were my family too! My aunt, my cousins, they are a part of my story.

Dad: I did not see it like that, it was my loss, I lost my sister, I loved my sister, I loved the boys and Carol, it broke my heart and I never thought I would allow myself to feel anything again. Then your mother came along and then you, it changed everything, and I needed to protect you.

Me: You cannot protect a child from the difficulties and the pain of life, that just is. Are you angry with me for breaking my promise?

Dad: Honestly, yes, I am, I was protecting you from it, and I wanted to protect my sister too, from your judgement, I wanted to preserve her for you, not as she was known but as she had been.

Me: But you didn't, did you? You never talked about her so I could not have what you had, a memory of a lovely woman who did something terrible, I was just left with the terrible bit. I feel cheated of her, deprived of her and the children too and that is what I am trying to redress here somehow. You had no right to ask that promise of me, no right at all, it was selfish of you to not allow me the chance to know this part of my family history.

Dad: I am sorry, I was in pain, and I put my pain before your needs, I am sorry.

Me: That is what I needed to hear. I have always put you on a pedestal and never addressed your selfishness, never dared to allow myself to see it and it has really affected me in this case. I needed to know you are sorry, I needed to know that you understand why I needed to do this. I have felt disloyal at times as I have begun to put my thoughts about all this in writing, but now I am doing something I need to do for me. I am prioritising the me over you for once, it is not us/we now, but me.

Dad: I was always proud of you, and I did tell you, but more than anything I am proud of how you are dealing with this. I wish I had trusted you with it, I wish I had talked to you about her so you could have really known her, not just her awful sin.

Me: You are the one wrapped up in sin, she was ill, Dad, she was ill and now she would have had support, but then there was nothing. She was a lost soul and ill and I do have a sense of her now, I am going to look at a time before it happened, and I am going to find her. I am not calling her a sinner but someone who did a dreadful thing one day that there was no coming back from, but I will not get into the blame game, I leave that to the rest of you.

Dad: Do you remember when we watched *Brideshead Revisited* together and that scene when Julia Flyte talks of carrying around her little sin, always there. I know you saw it had a huge effect on me, well, I feel I have been carrying my little sin of failing my sister and especially the children, I did not want to fail you, I just want to keep you safe.

Me: Let it go now, Dad, all this sin stuff, let it go. I forgive you; your sins are forgiven, your God forgave you long ago, now I forgive you too and I am sorry, I am so very sorry that your young life was blighted by this tragedy. Of course, I see your grief, your despair, I just needed to be allowed to acknowledge it with you, not share it with you, but have the opportunity to understand it. Can they all be allowed to be laid to rest now, can we finally close this chapter? I need to do that now Dad, I need to stop this dark story lurking behind corners to catch me, to inform my guilt, feed my blame, enhance my shame, I need it to stop now.

Dad: Yes, enough now, enough.

Experiencing this dialogue was incredibly powerful for me, I said things I would never have considered before, it felt cathartic and freeing to challenge my father's position, it is a sign that the separation has real foundations now and my father's suffering no longer needs to belong to me.

There are so many family situations where such a dialogue can be so very helpful, or the perhaps more familiar process of writing a letter to someone but not sending it. The feelings need a voice, and it is damaging to silence that voice. Too often when the feelings are allowed out it is with anger and rage which leads to defensiveness from the other person and no resolution, resolving it within ourselves is an important step.

Chapter twenty

INTEGRATION

ANCESTRAL TIMELINE

I realised as I was writing, that though I have
referred to my aunt throughout this work at my
aunt, I have done this purely to protect her name. I
usually refer to her when I speak of her or even
within my mind, just by her first name. I have in
fact never called her aunt or fully identified her as
my aunt until now. Maybe I should give you her
name now, as I leave the shame and blame behind,
even that protectiveness I thought I was achieving,
I leave it all behind now, her name was Marcelle,
my Aunt Marcelle.

I need to welcome her into my consciousness,
an equal to my maternal aunt and uncle, as a way
to release the shame and the blame, to restore her
to her place within the family and I need to meet
Carol, Graham and Keith, I need to have a sense of
them. This process of visualisation I will be using
has great power, as our mind does not differentiate

fact from fiction, it reacts to what it perceives whether from the inner or outer eye.

We can also consider what Norman Doidge points out in his book on neuroplasticity, that Freud believed healing trauma requires unconscious trauma to be brought into the conscious to alter the response to it. But what if the unconscious trauma is not yours? You do not have the memory to retrieve, in fact all you have is your own imaginings and interpretations of that atmosphere or culture of trauma.

I wanted to find a way to both retrieve and integrate a memory that was not mine, to disempower the trauma. I needed to find a way to connect with my missing family and try to fill in the blanks. I did not feel I could relive the actual trauma; I feel I have already come close to that in retrieving the real facts, but I wanted to visit the family before the tragedy happened to get a sense of them.

I am using here a version of timeline therapy but stretching it into an ancestral timeline:

Visualise a translucent pathway of light that represents your timeline moving ahead of you into the future and it stretches behind you into your past, at the point of your birth it becomes a series of lines, threads leading back into the past, into your ancestral lines, it has many, many branches, a network of veins threading into your family's past. Perhaps it might help to see a great wide river with tributaries branching off at different points, the main wide river being yourself and the tributaries those threads into other's lives before you.

You are picking the line you want to follow into the aspect of your family that you need to deal with and as you watch the line below you, you are following a tributary of that river, watching it weave into the past and there is a huge crater, a damaged area on that ancestral line, disrupting the flow of the water, the flow of life, and that is the trauma you have been dealing with, but we are navigating around that crater, we are travelling to a point before the trauma happened, go back beyond it, yes, to a time just before it happened. In this case today we are passing beyond that damaged piece of the timeline to Easter Sunday 1954.

It is that happy Easter weekend for the family of the Triggs, Uncle Bruce is home for a long weekend and Aunt Marcelle seems relaxed and more contented than usual, and my cousins are there, they have just come back from church. The children are excited as they will get their chocolate eggs now that they have been to Sunday School, but their father says they need to wait until after their lunch.

My aunt has been saving her coupons and they are having a joint of roast beef for this Sunday as it is a special day, only she knows this is the last Sunday roast for the family. She takes great care with the cooking; she is doing their favourite pudding.

I am on the doorstep, hesitating to ring the bell, to meet them at last, to let them into my mind, my life, my story. I find a big door knocker and I bang it loudly, no going back now. The door is opened by a big bluff man in flannel trousers, a white shirt with the sleeves rolled up, a tie neatly knotted, braces, I see the neatness of an ex-military man, a trimmed moustache, a wide smile, as he is being infected by his wife's good mood. I notice the greying of his hair at the temples, the slight balding at the crown of his head, he is older than he had seemed in my dreams over the years and friendlier too.

I am your niece, I say, we have not met. He takes my hand within both of his and invites me in, taking me into the kitchen where the children are already seated around a scrubbed wooden table, legs swinging back and forth restlessly as all they want now is their chocolate. I say hello to Carol, so little with her still chubby infant legs, a huge infectious smile and a shock of dark wavy hair, just like her mother. She seems very proud of her special floral Sunday dress. Keith, the eldest, slips down from his chair, he is wearing dark grey shorts with long socks and those Clark's sandals we all seemed to wear to primary school. He has a smart white shirt and even a tie. He walks over and soberly shakes my hand, as he is the eldest, he has to set the tone, his small warm hand in mine, I want to keep hold of it and keep him safe.

Now Graham, he is the image of his father, those slightly sticking out ears, and the fairer hair, there is a real playfulness about him, he has the shorts and the shirt but there is no sign of a tie. I feel myself smiling, I cannot help myself as the children chatter questions at me, where am I from? Am I staying for lunch? Did I bring any chocolate eggs?

My aunt turns and now, now I want to cry as I look into those dark eyes, hello Aunt, I am your niece, we have not met yet, I say, I have waited to meet you for so long. There is a feverishness about her, she is slightly flushed. Is that the heat from the oven or does it reflect her mood? She sweeps me into a big hug, she is thinner than I thought she would be, I can feel the bones of her shoulder blades and she is shorter.

I do not know why I had imagined she would be taller than me, but we are much the same height and frame, but she is thinner, she clearly has not been eating well. She invites me to join them at the table. There is the big joint of beef there and roast potatoes, Yorkshire pudding and some carrots, a traditional Sunday dinner. I doubt her mother taught her to do that! She is fulfilling her role as the English housewife. I sit at the table and join in the food; Graham will not eat his carrots and Keith is showing off teasing him as he has a new audience.

I ask the boys about their school and special friends, and they chatter away. Carol wants to get in on the act and tells me about how she helps mummy in the kitchen rolling pastry, though there is none today, as there is apple crumble for pudding, which Carol turns into a squidgy mess by stirring it around and around in the bowl. The attention span of the children has been exhausted by the excitement of their visitor and they whine about leaving the table and for some peace and quiet they are allowed to go to give my aunt a break. Uncle Bruce goes with them, I am left with Marcelle to help with the washing up.

The boys dash off to play with their matchbox toys and Carol is clutching a rather battered old doll. Bruce retires, has a cigarette, perhaps this is really behind his withdrawal. As I stand with my aunt at the sink, piles of plates around us, I glance sideways at her, not quite believing she is plotting her disastrous action, is she? Isn't she? I try to get her to talk about her life, but it meets with a blank, too much bottled up and this must be a special day, it is the last Sunday.

If I were a time traveller, could I change what happened here? I think not, the pattern is woven and fixed, all I can do is share this moment and try to get a sense of this aunt I never had the chance to meet. Maybe today was not the best day to choose, but I have gone through this now, I have put myself here. I could look into a different future to see what might have been, me being a bridesmaid at Carol's wedding, of course she would be much older than me in real time, going to the theatre with my aunt, a holiday in France together perhaps, all of us, but it does not help.

I see her in this flat far away from her family and all that she has known. What a fish out of water she is, she does not belong here, she is lost here, the scuffed linoleum on the floor, the several times patched and mended clothes, the worn look about the eyes. I see those continental dark circles under her eyes, that we both got from her father that no-one else seems to have. Am I still angry with her for taking the children from me? That is how I saw it once.

I see her now, scrubbing a plate, her hands red from the water, a piece of hair falling into her eyes as she blows it away, I can feel her distress just below the surface. All I want to do is hold her in my arms and tell her she is going to be ok, I want to hold her and not let her go, as if she were hanging over a precipice and if I just held on long enough, help would come and we could pull her up to safety, but I am exhausted already, just being in this house, the energy here is sapping and draining and it is all too late.

I am not angry now, but it is too much to suggest forgiving, it is not really something one can forgive, but perhaps I can understand she reached a breaking point. My sense of her is of someone about to snap and I get that, why did nobody see it? That is what I wonder as I watch her moving about her home with the tension of a coiled spring.

I have spent my life rescuing others, perhaps as I could not rescue her. I now have a new image of her, she is not fixed in that photo frame anymore. She has an essence which I feel, skin I can almost touch, I could even reach out and push that hair out of her eyes, it flops in that way rather like mine. I do feel at peace with her now, I have a sense of her, just like my father always wanted me to do. He did not want me to read about what she did, as he wanted me to know her for more than her final act. He always said to me 'no-one is as bad as the worst thing they have ever done'. I had not realised until this moment, that was all about her.

I know her now, I feel I do, so I can allow the feelings to be there and of course it hurts more than before, but I have let her in, not left her on the outside, she is a part of my life too now.

I go into the sitting room, Carol sits on her father's lap waving her doll under his nose, no wonder he said, 'the girl' at the inquest. How could he connect in that moment with his lovely little girl, the terrible loss. I get down on the floor with the boys and they show me their battered cars with great pride, though the paint is peeling off at the side, broom, broom we go, as we push them along the carpet to see who will win the race. My Morris Minor is doing quite well, ahead of Graham's Ford, but Keith's Austin wins, pips me to the finishing post. They tell me the cars were a present from Uncle Paul who will be coming to see them in a couple of weeks, but he is away at the moment, they chatter about what presents he might bring next time.

At least they had this day, this normal Easter Sunday, the wrappers of the Fry's Easter eggs screwed up and cast aside. I know I have to leave now; I have seen this from the inside, that perfect Easter weekend that Bruce described in that bewildered way. I need to go on my way, but just before I take my leave, I look over at him, who I had blamed all these years. Poor man, he was out of his depth with this woman, he tried to make her happy, thought another child might do the trick, desperate to make her happy, but not a clue what to do.

I bend down over the boys, still roaring up and down with their toy cars, and ruffle Keith's hair and plant a kiss on the top of Graham's head, then over to Bruce. I give him a hug this tall man with the roughened hands, perhaps from those years in the army, no I do not blame him anymore and if there is any blame to be had he paid the price a hundred times over, he lost these wonderful kids and he never again shared a family Sunday just like this. Carol last, a kiss on her warm plump cheek.

I need to go now, there are other things I need to do but not now, this was enough, as I breathe in the sea air on the doorstep and close the door quietly behind me and slip away, into my life today following the thread of a timeline down its tributary length back to my life, a little sadder perhaps but finally feeling complete. The missing pieces have found their place. But wait, I did not say goodbye to her, I realised I had left her in the kitchen, maybe I just cannot do it, I could not look into her eyes and say goodbye knowing what I was leaving her to do.

When I came out of this exercise, I was surprised it had not been more painful. I had tears in my eyes but I did not cry, I felt a deep connection to the children which I had not expected as my objective had been very much focused on Marcelle but she felt somehow unreachable, perhaps she was too troubled for me to allow myself to get too close, though that moment by the sink in the kitchen is very vivid to me and has stayed the sharpest single image from the experience.

I had a sense of Bruce's love for his kids and a slight bewilderment in him at how to cope with his rather exotic wife. I felt he never truly knew her but did the best he could for her, was perhaps aware he was failing. I said within the piece that I knew she was planning what she was going to do but of course she may not have been, though I had a sense of how lost she was. It was a very powerful and surprisingly good experience which contributed to my sense of closure on this family tragedy.

This kind of visualisation exercise when done in trance is very powerful, as you are working with the subconscious, it can lay down a new programme, a new connection in your mind. Rubin Battino touches upon this in *Metaphoria,* arguing that the differential between fantasy and reality is a challenge for the mind, the gap is imperceptibly small, the fantasy can become as a reality, and this is so powerful for healing the past.

We can begin to reframe the past and see it differently. If you are planning such an exercise, it must be done with a professional who will guide you through the process and be with you on that journey in case it becomes emotional. It is also a good idea to establish a safe place in the mind to retreat to, should you start to feel very emotional, as I explained earlier in this section.

Our memory of real events is just a recording laid down in the mind, which when we revisit it, we make it stronger and more vivid. Sometimes we misremember things and subtly alter the memory. That memory is still real to us, though others will not remember it in the same way. I may never have met the family, but this exercise has brought them to life for me, they are no longer hidden away and that is important in healing this past trauma for me.

It must be real to me, for me to be able to live with it rather than a phantom gifted to me by my father.

There is still some suspicion in certain quarters about the use of trance, which usually comes from a lack of knowledge or experience. Some have tried to circumvent this by repackaging hypnotherapy and self-hypnosis in a different guise, such as Dr Mike Dow's development of Subconscious Visualisation Therapy, which is a visualisation process in a light trance. It can be useful to use other terms to deliver the work that needs to be done, meditation, trance, all leading us into the subconscious to aid change.

A lot of the previous work is centred around the psychological impact of the trauma, for more physical issues a form of parts therapy can be very helpful.

PARTS THERAPY

Parts therapy enables the therapist to address the part of the individual that is creating the problem, whether that be a physical problem or a behaviour, to address why it is happening and to encourage that part to find a new way of achieving its goal. I often use the sentence with a client that they must find a new way to do for them, what 'it' used to do but does not do now, to direct them towards change, even consciously thinking that through can be helpful.

Some people feel uncomfortable with the idea of parts, as they worry about a sense of divided self which we see in schizophrenia, but what we are talking about is a less clear-cut division within the self. We all present different aspects of ourselves depending on where we are and what we are doing, a simplistic view would be that we are different at home with our family than how we might project ourselves at work. It is interesting how we can meet someone brimming with confidence in their workplace but cowed at home by their partner, decisive at work but indecisive at home.

It is this kind of alternative part or aspect of personality that we address during this therapeutic approach. In Neuro Linguistic Programming we see the argument that every behaviour has a purpose, even when that purpose can seem a bit distorted. I have worked with an IBS sufferer who was a mother in a busy family. When we worked with the part of her that was causing the IBS symptoms, it became clear that the time she spent in the bathroom in the morning was the only time she had to herself all day, so the symptom bought her some time, even though it brought with it a problem. Obviously, it would be easier for the said mother to assert her need for some time rather than suffer with IBS, but the mind generates creative responses to problems it does not want to confront.

Physical symptoms can have what we call secondary gains. It is our job to find out that gain and find a way to provide it without needing the illness. It can be the same for certain behaviours too. There can be a lot of resistance within this kind of therapy, and it is important to persist to reach the hidden desire/need/purpose.

Now we will look at a script following a version of parts therapy. I went through this process with a colleague, and it was surprisingly short, it would usually take a lot longer to reach the cause. I have worked with hypnotherapy for so many years I conclude that perhaps I am very receptive to the process. So, I present it here as an example, but have not included the trance induction that was used:

Questioner: Would the part of you that is responsible for creating these symptoms be present?

Me: Yes.

Q: How old is she?

Me: About seven or eight.

Q: Tell me what you can see, why is she created?

Me: I am about seven years old, and I want to help my grandma, her head is nodding, she is not happy, she is reading a letter whilst sitting at her dressing table. The letter is telling her that her sister has died of cancer. I want to help her; she is clearly very upset *(Her sister had lived for many years in Australia, so they had not seen each other for a long time though they wrote often.)* She is very sad, and I want to help her, she is often sad. No, she is always sad.

Q: Is nodding your head like her going to help her?

Me: I do not know what to do to help her, I love her and I want to ease the sadness, I want her to see I am here for her.

Q: Matching what she is doing, how does that help her?

Me: I do not know.

Q: Is there something else you could do for her instead?

Me: I do not know what to do, I feel helpless in face of her sadness, I feel sad too now.

Q: Can we see that this moment has moved into the past and she is at peace now, so she does not need you to nod, to share her suffering anymore.

She is no longer here, she does not need you to do this now, it is after all too late to be doing that now. What can you do now instead if you want to do something for her?

Me: I can go to her grave and clear it up, I can do that for her now.

Q: Can you come to terms with this now? Do you realise you do not need to help her once you have cared for the grave?

Me: I want to do that and see how it feels. I want to let that confused and troubled part that did not know how to help my grandma, be at peace now.

As I noted, this was a surprisingly brief, with clear exchanges when I did it. As I did not nod my head at eight years old, it is surprising I am considering that is where the part that created it originated. Perhaps it is simply that is when I noticed my grandmother's sadness first in a powerful way.

The extra loss of her sister which I had not remembered until I did this exercise had resurrected for her the other losses and I had sensed this, and I wanted to help her. My father had taken on the shaking after she died though only with his hands. Now they are both gone, I may be showing the family sadness in this way, I am taking on the grief of all the family sadness and this is what I had learned at a subconscious level. Returning to the grave seems a good way to try to get some resolution anyway and I had wanted to do it, this is a reminder that the time has come to do so.

Chapter twenty-one

RETURNING TO THE GRAVE

It is time now to return. I can understand now why I did not go back before, I needed to know the real story and then complete these therapeutic processes to face the whole story, for it to be a real connection for me. I want to put flowers upon Marcelle and the children's grave now that I know who they really are, my family. I needed to also understand that there was this one last thing I could to do for my grandmother at her grave.

It is quite a pilgrimage, as the cemetery is a round trip of around six hours, so it needed to be planned and prepared for. As the day dawned the sky was blue, no wind, a perfect spring day, two weeks before the anniversary of their deaths, that was not exactly part of the plan it was just the time my partner and I could go, but felt very apt. As we arrive, it is deserted, a Sunday, we expect many people to be around, but we see just one other person tending a grave, busily digging and planting, otherwise it is quiet and still.

The first thing I do is pay more attention this

time. When I came before, I was overwhelmed by the reality of being there, at acknowledging this was not a story made up to justify the sadness of my family, but a real one, Marcelle and the children had existed, there they were down in the ground.

It took some time to find the grave again, it was more damaged, some twine holding the headstone upright, making it seem even more sad. I paid more attention this time, taking it all in.

So, I read the inscription *In Loving Memory of My Dear Wife Marcelle and My Three Lovely Children, Keith, Graham and Carol, Ever in Daddy's Thoughts'*. I was already considering these words again when I received Bruce's death certificate earlier in my quest, I was struck even more seeing the grave for a second time, his reference to his dear wife, he could still put this endearment in stone, set there in perpetuity, for all to see. He must have truly loved her, maybe he did understand her pain. I was in that moment deeply touched with pity for this man.

The first time I came it was all about my connection to my aunt, I had wanted to find her, this enigmatic woman in the photograph, then I became absorbed by the story of the missing children. As I stood looking down at the grave, I could not leave my uncle out of the picture any longer, I was overwhelmed by the sense of his loss.

I began to imagine more clearly the day of that

funeral in 1954 when mother and children were laid to rest, a small group gathered around, both sets of grandparents, my father and Bruce, possibly siblings of Bruce if he had any, all gathered around. How did they stand upright? Bracing themselves against the loss, how were they not doubled up in agony at the senseless theft of life? I see Bruce, an ex-army man, British, stiff upper lip, as his beloved wife and three children were lowered into the ground. Four coffins. One atop the other. Which order did they go in? I imagine little Carol in last, the smallness of the coffin cutting deep into the hearts of the family.

I see my tiny grandmother held up by her husband, holding it together for their remaining child, setting the example he would follow, lock the pain away, lock it away, lock it all away. I think of him then, my father, just 24, and realise he would have still been a child when his first nephew was born. I feel it must have made them seem close, maybe more like younger siblings to him, that were buried that day, with the sister he had idolised and revered. I think more about his relationship with the children, how the boys would have looked up to him when he went off to do his military service in L'Armee de L'air, like a big brother to boast about, they would have wanted to see his uniform.

My father once told me a story of sneaking his uniform out of France which was not allowed, maybe that was why he did so, when he was on leave that time, breaking all the rules, hiding it beneath his pyjamas and a batch of dirty washing in case he was searched, to show them, his adoring nephews. I will never know for sure, all I can ever do is imagine, but it gives some sense to that old story.

How did they survive that day I wonder, as I see them in my mind's eye, trying to stand upright and not bend into the pain?

Back to today, I lay my flowers. How long since this grave has seen flowers? Decades, I guess. My grandparents are not far away, but that day in 1982 when we laid grandma to rest, we did not come here, I did not know they were just two minutes' walk away, I could have known them then. I have wondered whether my father slipped away that day to look at the grave, or whether it was all too tightly locked up for him. I stand looking down, more connected than before as I know their story now, not a family myth, but real people who lived and breathed and carried my DNA.

The wording on the graves is falling away, metal letters pressed into light engravings, the first letter of my aunt's name has fallen off. My partner picks it up and presses it into my hand, a moving gesture that almost breaks me down, but I clutch it tight and walk away.

And onto my grand parents' grave, this I tackle with unrestrained vigour, to pull back the encroaching grass. I tug and I pull and I dig, to reveal their long neglected names, I talk to grandma as I dig, 'sorry it has been so long, this is the least I can do for you, you loved me so much, I want you to know I am fine, despite the head nodding just like you, I am happy and safe, no need to worry about me, I am strong, just like you'.

When the plaque is free of the grass, I rub it down with water making the names clear and readable and I lay some flowers there. You are not forgotten, never forgotten.

As I look around the many neglected graves, but focus in on those that belong to me, I hope I give them remembrance in my words, and that those who have shared this journey with me will remember them too. I send a photo of the grave with the flowers to my mentor Maureen. 'Bless them' she says.

As I reach the end of this work, I feel changed, the writing I have already said has been therapeutic, but the work I have done as a part of this journey has led to significant change, I feel stronger than ever before, stronger in mind and body. I do not know if I can turn back the tide on my physical symptoms or at least halt them, but I can say that I have had some improvement.

My head tremors are happening much less already, and I recently walked up the side of a mountain clutching my snow poles and wearing crampons, a feat that I would have felt way beyond my physical strength and sense of balance a few months ago, so who knows? I am so glad to have taken the skeleton out of the cupboard and polished it, I feel it was long overdue.

As you have shared my journey with me, I hope it has shed some light on your own life, your family past and present, encouraged you to look into the nooks and crannies of your family cupboard and consider tackling what you find there.

Chapter twenty-two

ENDINGS AND BEGINNINGS

THE GIFT OF A DREAM

As I drew towards the end of writing this book and the therapeutic work that accompanied it, I had a powerful dream. In this dream I was holding my grandmother's hand, it was warm and soft within my grasp, and I was looking intently into her eyes. It felt such a strong connection, it felt so real that when I awoke, I could still feel her hand in mine, I could feel her presence as if she were there. I am not referencing this as something ghostly or esoteric, but as a point of peace within my mind with my grandmother.

It reminded me of her warmth, how tactile she was and how safe she had made me feel, but it also felt like I had absolution for writing about my family, not from her of course, that is not possible, but to myself via her, a way I needed to experience it and experiencing this as a dream rather than a pure conscious thought, it had greater resonance, more power, deep into my mind.

There is one other thing that has changed in my life, the very observant reader might notice my imprecise language in reference to partners past and present, in a way seemingly unlinked to the trauma, but perhaps it comes through as inherited shame or a reflection of the times I grew up in, but I hesitate to mention the gender of my partner and now I feel I have a right to say my partner is a woman.

My parents were always very supportive of my relationships, but I still somehow felt difficulty in the writing to be direct about it, as I reach the end of my story no more secrets.

POSTSCRIPT TO MY STORY

No sooner have I got to the end of my story when another bombshell explodes in my family, another secret that has been squirrelled away. I open an email from a cousin of my father and try very hard to understand the contents. His DNA has matched to the daughter of an old friend of my father from the long distant past. I struggle to compute the information until I realise, he is saying she is my half-sister, DNA does not lie.

My narrative of this only child with her special relationship with her father, the father she idolised has had a rather icy bucket of water dowsed over it, as I can no longer see him as the perfect man that I once did. I am glad I had done the separation work around my father before I had found out about it, as it puts me in a stronger position to process this. I wonder if you also notice, I am no longer the end of the line for that family from Normandy, the genes have found their way through another way, nature will have its say. I have two nephews who will never carry my father's name, but the genes go on and the story of the family continues. I cannot imagine that he knew, but I will never know for sure.

I had an image in my mind when I thought about it, of a devastated bomb site with green shoots poking up through the rubble, there is life after tragedy.

I have met my sister and my nephews, and they are truly lovely, all the initial shock faded away the moment we met. This was another family secret, and I am so glad that it came out into the light, it feels like my father left me a gift beyond the grave. Thank you, Dad, I can say that now, thank you.

Chapter twenty-three

RESOLUTION

Reading about the potential impact of trauma on families and how it affected mine, may have triggered something in you, making you aware that there is an unresolved trauma in your own family.

This trauma can be caused by a whole range of experiences at a personal level, such as sexual assault, rape, murder, missing persons, and accidents, these all carry with them the potential for trauma that can ripple out beyond the bounds of the affected person and into other generations. The most common cause I encounter within my therapeutic work is suicide. The guilt at not saving the person will affect most people who are left behind, even when they have realistically done all that they can to keep the loved one here and this is easily transmitted to others. There is also, sadly, sometimes a sense of shame clinging to the family.

I use a metaphor with my clients who are wrestling with this. I equate it to someone being in a room with you and they want to leave the room. We can bar the door to stop them, we can wrestle them to the ground to keep them there, we can try to keep watch twenty-four hours a day, but eventually they will evade our vigilance. We cannot keep them in that room forever and we can consider whether we even have a right to do so.

We may love that room and want them to stay there with us as we love them too, but if they do not feel the same about it, they have free will, they are an individual with their own rights.

If they are suffering, should we make them stay for our own sake? We still do not acknowledge enough the depth of suffering that someone must be feeling to take such action, total agony that could be compared to the physical pain of someone dying of cancer. That does not mean we do not do all that we can to help someone who is suffering, but there comes a point, just as with some cases of terminal cancer, where that battle may fail.

Trauma can feel like something that happens to other people, other families, but it can affect real people, people like you and me. Every time you read a newspaper headline about a suicide or a rape for example, there is a family being ripped apart by trauma.

So, what can you do if now you feel that it is affecting your family? You can see from my therapeutic journey that there are many things that can be done, ideally within a therapeutic setting, but you can begin the healing yourself.

BREAK THE SECRECY

The first and most important thing to do is to address the secrecy. From all I have written in this book, the clearest message must be that secrecy is harmful as it fuels the guilt, blame and shame running through the family and can lead to distortions of events. This distortion of events makes them harder to process, as you are not dealing with reality. I come back to the idea of fighting shadows; we need to bring the true story into the light.

You may meet resistance when you begin to take the lid off what has happened in your family, if you do meet such resistance, you might need to do this in group therapy, but the secrecy needs to go, it helps no-one. Some things that may help you are outlined below.

TELL YOUR STORY

A way to begin this process is to write your own story in just the same way as I have done, revisit the past of your family, painful as that may be at times and tell your understanding of that story. Imagine you are meeting someone for the first time, and they want to know you, what shaped you and made you who you are. I am not suggesting this for a direct trauma, something that has happened to you, but something within the family, not in your generation perhaps, that has affected the behaviour of everyone in the family.

It does not need to be as detailed as what I have written, but tell the facts and reflect at the same time on how you think it may have affected other family members.

Set the scene first, where you are in your family? An only child, one of many, where do you sit in that family? What was your role within the family? The joker, the peacemaker, the rebel, the nurturer? Did your role change over time?

How did you relate to your parents? Were you closer to one that the other and if so, why do you think that was?

Look at your wider family, grandparents, aunts, uncles, and cousins, how did you relate to them? Were you closer to your maternal or paternal family? If so, why do you think that was?

Pick out some key moments that might have affected you and consider why they were so significant for you.

How was school for you, did you thrive, wither, or just drift through without it impacting much upon you?

After you have considered your formative years, what brought you to where you are now? Describe your current family situation, life situation and consider how the trauma in your family may have impacted on your decisions, choice of partner, perhaps even job, types of friends.

When you have finished this work, you may then wish to share your story with other family members or get them to write their version of events. This may enable you to break this secrecy and open a dialogue. It may surprise you how different even siblings' perception of events can be. We influence our recounting of a story with our own personality and the position from which we have experienced events, whether older or younger, you may have been more, or less protected by what happened. To hear the story from different family members perspectives will help you to understand their feelings.

Every time we relive a memory in our mind, we may just alter it a little and it can become over time very different from the original experience, so checking in with another family member who may be altering their mental record too, is a useful thing to do. It is important to do this in a peaceful, non challenging way, so ask them how it was for them, they need to feel they can be heard too. It may in fact surprise you what they say, it may be very different to the role you have assigned for them in your head.

We have to remember that nobody is a mind reader, they may have no idea that their actions have impacted on you at all. When I first discussed how I felt Marcelle and the children's deaths had affected me, it was met with great surprise, until I calmly explained how it had impacted on the actions of everyone in the family and therefore it had affected me.

The person most affected by a trauma becomes so involved in dealing with it that their capacity to be aware of other people's experiences are very dimmed. In most cases there is no mal intent, just an inability to cope with a situation which prevents them from seeing another's point of view.

We also need to understand that there is a purpose behind our actions, every behaviour has a purpose no matter how irrational that purpose might seem on reflection. This exercise may help you to understand the purpose behind the actions of your other family members. People rarely mean real harm, though actions can be misguided and lead to harm unintentionally. You may be still judging the situation from a child's perspective; you can now bring to that an adult interpretation. It is also important to hold onto the fact, that how someone behaves in one moment is not the sum of who they are. After all, none of us wants to be judged by one action in one moment in time, we are much more than that.

WRITE TO YOUR YOUNGER SELF

An approach we often pursue in hypnotherapy involves visiting the younger part of the self within trance, that part needed support but did not get it at the critical time. When we are a child or teenager we feel very alone with our fears, and we feel we are the first person that has ever felt such fears. Events can feel very out of proportion, we feel nobody understands us and being understood is so very important, particularly when we are young, it makes us feel safe and that we belong.

A way you can work with this outside of trance, is to write a letter to the younger part of yourself. It will help this process if you have a picture of yourself at the age you feel you most needed support. Now imagine you can communicate with this child; you are a time traveller, you can take this letter back in time. What does this younger you need to hear; how can you support them?

I would suggest they need to know that they have survived this difficult time they are experiencing, tell them this and tell them the good things that have happened to you since then.

The mind is prone to a negative bias, we need to try to counter this by writing down all the good bits and tell the younger self they have all these great things to look forward to in the future.

If it seems relevant, you may want to outline events or improved relationships with other family members if this has happened.

Tell your younger self they are loved and that you are there for them, the special friend, advocate they needed at that time but did not have. Tell them that you understand how they feel.

It may be useful to ask a friend to read this letter to you or record it on your phone or a recording device and listen to it. If you do such a thing, do it when you have some quiet time to yourself and not when you are busy doing something like driving, you need to be able to close your eyes and take it in.

WHAT CAN YOU USE FROM MY THERAPY EXPERIENCE?

You may want to use some of the ideas that I have outlined in my own therapy process as simple visualisation exercises. Those that can be adapted to a range of experiences would be the 'boundaries on the beach' to help you establish strong boundaries, 'the coat' to find which learnings from your family you wish to keep and those you wish to discard. The 'playing cards exercise' to release feelings may also be a useful starting point for you and there are clear instructions in the text. As recommended with the other exercises, recording and listening to the scripts can be very helpful.

You may as an alternative want to write a dialogue like that which I did for my father, especially if the person is no longer alive, it gives you the chance to reflect on what their responses might be to your experience.

This book is designed to bring an understanding and awareness about the possibility of inheriting trauma within your family and ways in which it might affect you. I wanted to leave you with some ideas that could help you begin to understand your own experience and begin that process of resolution and healing. You can then help to prevent that trauma continuing down the generations, it can stop with you, you have the power to break that pattern.

Even the awareness that you have been affected by inherited trauma will help you to address the issues caused by it.

There is a list of organisations at the end of the book that will provide help to find a suitable therapist if you feel you need some professional support.

Acknowledgements

This book would not have been written without the encouragement and support of my mentor Maureen Williams. When I began to talk to her about this story and how I felt it had affected me she said, 'You must write about this'. She did not say maybe, or perhaps, but you must and so it began, tentatively at first and then it turned into a flow of expression and exploration that has been an incredible journey. I checked in with her frequently to discuss how it was developing and she said to me 'You are on a journey, imagine you are on a train and I am the guard at the stations along the way that you check in with, to check that you are on the right train, the right place on the journey, those stations may be close together or far apart it is up to you'.

As someone who sees metaphors as the most powerful way of communicating and indeed healing, this metaphor spoke to me and I thank her for being such a good guide on my journey, always there in the background for me to call upon in those sometimes-wobbly moments and sometimes very excited ones!

The other constant on this journey with me was my partner Evelyn Meyer, who read and re-read draft after draft, who listened to my ideas and interpretations of events and came up with alternative views and her own insightful interpretations, as ever, she made me think and supported me. The day that the researcher sent through the inquest information, something I had waited years to read, she was 800 miles away and could not be with me, so she suggested I email it to her, she would read it first just in case there was anything in there she thought I would not cope with and then we would read it together. This was the right thing to do, it helped me so much for someone to be in a sense with me and she stayed with me all the way through to the last full stop in this book.

This has been hard for my mother, for me to drag this all up after my father has died. I think she hoped all of this had been buried with him. At first, I think she could not see that something that had happened before I was born could have affected me at all, but as I explained, she began to understand and helped me in any way she could, allowing me to talk through painful memories with her. I am so grateful to her. I think it has been very good for our relationship and helped me to understand how difficult at times it must have been for her. I hope that my exploration of this story has helped her to understand how it had impacted on her life too.

I would not have found the information on the family that I needed without the help of Elizabeth Yule, a researcher in Canterbury, who not only found me the information I needed, but handled it sensitively, referring to what a tragedy this was for my family. I appreciated this acknowledgement very much, as I hovered over the keys to finally see the real story that had been hidden for so many years. It is so interesting how powerful a thoughtful word from a stranger can be.

Several colleagues have helped me with the therapeutic work, Louise Matthews, Julie Adams, Rebecca Northfield and Mia Pal discussed the therapeutic approaches and helped deliver some of the scripts, bracing themselves for abreactions that surprisingly never came. Thanks to 'The Positivity Therapists' for their help with the book title and John Christian Jacques for his work on the photograph.

My warmest thanks also to my cousins Jane German and Isobel Williams for trawling through family memories and to friends who patiently listened as I began to tell a story that they had not known about. Everyone I have spoken to has shown compassion for Marcelle and not judged her, for which I am truly grateful.

Thank you.

References for Part Two

Chapter One

Grandchildren of Survivors: Can Negative Effects of Prolonged Exposure to Excessive Stress be Observed Two Generations Later? John J Sigal Ph.D Vincenzo F Dinicola M.D, Michael Buonvino B.A. Canadian Journal of Psychiatry. First Published April 1, 1988 (Abstract)

From Generation to Generation, Healing Transgenerational trauma through story-telling, Emily Wanderer Cohen. Morgan James Publishing, page 14
Ibid., 41

Lifting the blankets: The transgenerational effects of trauma in Indigenous Australia. PhD thesis. Judy Atkinson 2001. Queensland University of Technology

The Aftermath of Combat-Related PTSD: Toward an Understanding of Transgenerational Trauma, Melissa Pearrow and Lisa Cosgrove. Communication disorders Quarterly
First Published September 5, 2008

Belonging, Nora Krug. Simon and Schuster

Soft Wired, Dr Michael Merzenich. Parnassus Publishing, page 74-75

Chapter Two

Transgenerational Trauma and Therapy – The Transgenerational Atmosphere Tihamér Bahó and Katalin Zana. Routeledge, page 30

Lost in Transmission, Studies of Trauma Across Generations, Edited by M. Gerard Fromm. Routeledge, pages xx, xxi
Ibid., Loenburg 55

Haunting Legacies, Violent Histories and Transgenerational Trauma, Gabrielle Schwab. Columbia University Press, page 77
Ibid., 119

Chapter Three

Transgenerational Trauma and Therapy – The Transgenerational atmosphere, Tihamér Bahó and Katalin Zana, Routeledge, page 95
Ibid., 9

Haunting Legacies, Violent Histories and Transgenerational Trauma, Gabrielle Schwab

Columbia University Press, page 79
Transgenerational Trauma and Therapy – The Transgenerational Atmosphere, Tihamér Bahó and Katalin Zana. Routeledge, page 13/14

Chapter Four

Working with persistent physical symptoms and the physical response to trauma using hypnotherapy and EMDR K Chartres, Katherine Chartres Nurse Consultant NTW.NHS Foundation Trust.

Placebo effect statistics 2020-2021 Data, examples and indications, Arthur Zuckerman May 2020 Compare camp

Labelling of medication and placebo alters the outcome of episodic migraine attacks, Slavenka Kam-Hanson, Mosha Jakubowski, John M Kelley, Irving Kirsch, David C Hoaglin, Ted J Kaptchuk, Rami Burstein, SCI Trans med 2014 Jan 8 6(218)

The Placebo Response, Howard Brody. Journal of Family Practice, vol 49 issue 7

Is the Nocebo affect hurting your health? Serusha Govender, Web MD (www.webmd.com)

When the Body Says No, Gabor Mate. Penguin Random House, page 201
Ibid., 225

Chronic Pain Types Differ in Their Reported Prevalence of Post-Traumatic Stress Disorder (PTSD) and There Is Consistent Evidence That Chronic Pain Is Associated with PTSD: An Evidence-Based Structured Systematic Review David A. Fishbain, MD, FAPA, Aditya Pulikal, MD, JD, John E. Lewis, PhD, Jinrun Gao, MS, MBA Pain Medicine, Volume 18, Issue 4, April 2017, page 711–735

*Trauma and medically unexplained symptoms towards an integration of cognitive and neuro-biological account*s. Karin Roelofs Philip Spinhoven Clinical Psychology Review 2007 Oct;27(7):798-820.

The Brain that Changes Itself, Norman Doidge. Penguin, page 218-221

The Molecular Biology of Memory Storage: A Dialogue Between Genes and Synapses E R Kandel 2003 Nobel Lectures Physiology or Medicine 1996-2000 World Scientific Publishing Company, page 402

Chapter Five

The Genie in Your Genes, Dawson Church Energy
Psychology Press, page 75

The Biology of Belief, Bruce Lipton. Hay House

The Genie in your Genes, Dawson Church Energy
Psychology Press, page 290
Ibid., 298
Ibid., 52

The Biology of Belief, Bruce Lipton. Hay House,
page 144
Ibid., 142
Ibid., 161

*The public reception of putative epigenetic
mechanisms in the transgenerational effects of
trauma, Environmental epigenetics* 2018, 1-7
Rachel Yehyuda, Amy Lehmer and Linda M
Bierer

*Transgenerational Trauma and Therapy The
Transgenerational Atmosphere* Tihamér Bahó and
Katalin Zana. Reflections section, Dezsö Németh .
Routeledge Publishing, page 95

Chapter Six

From Generation to Generation, Healing Transgenerational Trauma Through Story-Telling, Emily Wanderer Cohen. Morgan James Publishing, page xvi

Chapter Seven

Self-Mastery Through Conscious Auto-Suggestion, Emile Coue. Digireads.com, page 22

Hypnotherapy, Dave Elman. Westwood Publishing, page 41

Chapter Eight

Family Constellations Revealed, Indra Torsten Preiss. Amazon, page 12

Schäm dich!, Matthias Kreienbrink, Die Zeit 04/2023

Blaming, Brene Brown YouTube: https://youtu.be/-mjyPFUg96o

Chapter Nine

Loyalty implications of the Transference Model,
Ivan   Boszormenyi-Nagy.   Arch   Gen
Psychiatry. 1972;27(3):374-380.

Chapter Ten

Metaphoria Rubin Battino M.S.   Crown House
Publishing, page 1-7

Chapter Eleven

It Didn't Start with You, Mark Wolynn. Penguin,
page 63
Ibid., 66

*Preventing   Intergenerational   Trauma
Transmission: A critical interpretive synthesis*.
Melinda Goodyear, Trentham Furness and Kim
Foster.
JCN 16 December 2018

*Transgenerational Trauma and Therapy, The
Transgenerational Atmosphere*, Tihamér Bahó
and Katalin Zana. Routledge, page 72/73
Ibid., 32

Chapter Twelve

The New Diary, Tristine Raynor. Tarcher/Putnam Books, page 119

The Brain That Changes Itself, Norman Doidge. Penguin, page 225

Metaphoria, Rubin Battino. Crown House Publishing, page 7

Your Subconscious Can Change Your Life, Dr Mike Dow. Penguin Random House

Useful Contacts

Hypnotherapy

UK Confederation of Hypnotherapy Organisations
www.ukcho.co.uk

British Association of Therapeutic Hypnosis
www.bathh.co.uk

Psychology Today
www.psychologytoday.com

Counselling and Psychotherapy

British Association of Counselling and
Psychotherapy
www.bacp.co.uk

American Psychological Association
www.apa.org

Urgent Assistance

Samaritans
www.samaritans.org
Call 116123

Samaritans USA
www.samaritansusa.org